D0699467

10

Unsung Heroes
OF
American Industry

Unsung Heroes

OF

American Industry

STORIES

Mark Jude Poirier

talk miramax books

Copyright © 2001 by Mark Jude Poirier

ISBN: 0-7868-6827-9

10.19.2003 Powells - Portland OR

For James G. Conley, III
and Mary Beth Fargo

Acknowledgments

Thanks to Diana Ossana for help and advice with all these stories. Michael Griffith and Greg Baxter at the *Southern Review* did a wonderful job with "Worms." Thanks to them. Thanks to Larry McMurtry and the rest of the staff at Booked Up in Archer City, and to the Louisiana State University Department of English, for providing me with great places to work while I wrote this book. I'm lucky to have Hilary Bass, Jin Auh, and Sarah Chalfant taking care of business for me in New York. Thanks. Beverly Wachtel helped with "Buttons" by taking me to cool places in Iowa and reading many drafts. Thanks. Finally, Jeff and Brandy, thanks for letting me sleep in your basement for months at a time.

"Worms" first appeared in the *Southern Review*. "Gators" first appeared in *Black Warrior Review*.

Contents

Unsung Heroes
OF
American Industry

Buttons

Visitors first see a series of large-scale ceramic structures that detail the biology of freshwater mussels. The three-foot mucket larva encysting itself on the gill of a salamander is bathed in a lurid red light that accentuates its underdeveloped excurrent siphon—a short tube that's curved into a grin, lips and all, but as guests read on the plaque below, actually functions like an anus. The hands-on area allows museum visitors to handle shells and identify mussel species from the Mississippi: Wabash pig-toes, creek heel-splitters, monkey-faces, winged maple-leafs, pimple-backs . . .

The west wall of the museum is devoted to the Badde Family, once known as the Royal Family of Pearl

Button Making. Faded black-and-white photographs feature the Baddes among their factory workers, hunched over trays of finished buttons, or sorting shells from a conveyer belt. One photo shows dapper brothers Thomas and Zilo Badde hosting the variety show at the Button Days Festival in 1947. That year's Miss Pearl Button stands alongside them, grins strenuously, tosses button samples into the crowd.

No part of the Badde history after the Great Button Crash in the 1950s is presented on the wall.

But the docent, who wears dark glasses, will recount post–Crash Badde Family history to any visitor who'll listen.

In 1965, Zilo Badde II was forced to move his family—his wife, Georgia, his sister-in-law, Trudie, and his three children: Zilo III, Susan, and Sandra—from here in Muscatine, Iowa, over a thousand miles west to southern Arizona. When the Japanese started to mass-produce plastic buttons in 1956, his family's pearl button company began to lose money rapidly. And besides, three consecutive seasons of skitter-worm plague had rendered half the mussels in the Mississippi rubbery, stinky flaps of floating, gray tissue—useless for button making. One of his employees, a shell accountant, waxed enthusiastic about Arizona, how everyone there was rich, living off copper-mining money in new stucco homes with peanut-shaped swimming pools they could use nine months out of the year. Zilo II had thought he could sell his family's button-making equipment, machines his father had designed and built himself. But he couldn't even *give* away the polishing tumblers, grinding wheels, or classifying instruments. No one wanted them. All things associated with pearl buttons were sad reminders to Muscatinites of a time that passed as quickly as it came.

Lucky for us, the town elders had the foresight to enlist the high-school football team in stowing a few button machines in the basement of the town hall, which is why they're here in the museum today.

The Button Boom of the early twentieth century had been a mirthful, prosperous time in this town. Summers brought hordes of hearty young men and women from all over the Lower Mississippi Valley to camp along the river. They spent their days in small boats, trolling for clams with special river-bottom-dragging implements called "crowfoots"—which were, of course, designed by the original Zilo Badde. As the sun set, the clam trollers would dock their boats, pull in the crowfoots, and descend upon Muscatine, crowding the taverns and dance halls.

Before Zilo II moved his family, he sold the emptied Badde Button Factory to an out-of-town businessman who turned it into a roller rink, which soon closed. A few years later, hippie artists bought the defunct rink and used it as cooperative gallery space for their psychedelic paintings. When a well-connected New York coed was found dead in the studio, sprawled on a soiled mattress under a butterfly mural, the hippies vacated.

Bored, the more diplomatic visitors will excuse themselves at this point. Others, intrigued by the docent's mysterious dark glasses and demeanor, will press for more information about the Badde family just so they can continue to watch him.

Today, the factory is a dilapidated storage facility for retreaded tires. It's only three blocks west of the museum. You'll see it on your right as you drive out of town.

This is tragic, if you consider that in 1943, *American Laundry Digest* featured a four-page spread on the Badde Button Company, in which they called Badde Buttons "the toughest and most attractive pearl buttons in the country." Even more tragic: The Badde Button Company was once responsible for thirty-six percent of all American freshwater pearl buttons manufactured. That was in 1939. In '48, the Badde Button Company produced twenty-eight percent. Not once in the forty-nine years of business did the percentage fall below nineteen.

The docent pauses. Sniffs. He guides the visitors to the rear of the museum, where an exhibit begins with a black-and-white mounted poster of Zilo Badde and the raised plastic words: ENTREPRENEUR, INVENTOR, GENIUS. If one of the visitors wants to know more, if he or she asks relevant and intelligent questions and doesn't make fun of Zilo Badde's wide-set amphibious eyes, if his or her own eyes are full of hope and compassion, the docent will offer a chair next to his metal desk up front, and continue with the Badde family history.

Zilo II never mined copper in Arizona, but instead opened a large chicken farm southeast of Tucson in the Rincon Mountains. He had bought the chicken farm from a Navajo man for next to nothing, and exercised the same Badde business profiency that his forefathers had. Within a year, it was the top egg-producing plant west of the Mississippi.

Two generations later, Zilo IV dug around the Tucson Public Library, typing "pearl buttons" and "Muscatine, Iowa" into the information systems, Xeroxing, printing, cross-referencing—while his twin brother Tommy socialized and pursued athletics.

• • •

"Wait," the museum visitors, say. "You skipped two Badde Family generations."

"Chickens and eggs," the docent says. "Just chickens and eggs."

Like visitors to this museum, Zilo IV was intrigued by his grandfather's financial sense and his great-grandfather's knack for invention. The pearl-button-polishing process that Zilo I had invented, where revolving kegs of pumice, hydrochloric acid, sawdust, and friction transformed the crude circles of clam shell into lustrous pearl buttons, had earned him a short entry in his great-grandson's favorite book: *The Unsung Heroes of American Industry.*

"Your great-grandfather's inventions didn't stop at pearl buttons," Zilo II—Grandpa—told Zilo IV one hot afternoon as they collected eggs in the colossal henhouse. They examined the shell membranes under microscopes—a treat for Zilo IV. "He invented ChapStick before the ChapStick company did. Mixed ground-up mussel shells with petroleum jelly and sap from river oaks. All the trollers had green lips that summer."

Zilo IV's father, Zilo III, a wan man, spent his days slumped in an air-conditioned cubicle above the egg house, talking on the phone, pecking at his keyboard.

Zilo IV didn't understand his father, was disappointed that his father wasn't inventing something or actively working to expand the family's business. Grandpa told Zilo IV that he had heard entrepreneurial genius skips every third generation, and that he was counting on Zilo IV and his twin, Tommy, to carry on the Badde family traditions.

Zilo IV was unpopular in school. He was called Chicken-Boy, or Egg-Boy—epithets perpetuated by the foul-smelling egg sandwiches he ordinarily brought for lunch. He kept to himself, ignored most of his classmates, and participated in no sports. He couldn't ignore his twin brother, Tommy, though. Tommy was seven minutes younger, and quite a charmer, even as a toddler, reciting the Pledge of Allegiance from on top of the coffee table.

Grandpa always invited Tommy to the egg house, whereas Zilo IV had to ask, and was often met with "Why isn't Tommy here to see this?" Grandpa attended all of Tommy's sporting events and cheered loudly, yelled "Show 'em you're Badde! Show 'em you're Badde, Tommy!" Zilo IV and Tommy were the only young Baddes; Aunt Susan and Aunt Sandra were homely and unmarried. Fortunately, from an early age, both Zilo IV and Tommy expressed interest in the family business— Zilo IV more explicitly.

Zilo IV spent his spare time in the library, hiding

from Tommy's bully friends who liked to punch the wind out of him. He read hundreds of books—mostly about inventors and zoology. In high school, he watched other students from behind fat calculus and physics tomes, convincing himself that their lives, full of juvenile high jinks and intrigue, were nothing to envy.

In the spring of his junior year at Canyon del Oro High, Zilo IV took the SAT.

Opening the mailbox in June was like opening an oven—the heat was palpable. But there, under a few bills, sat a large envelope from ETS in Princeton, New Jersey. A 1590. Almost perfect. He'd missed one, and even though he'd expected it, he was enraged. He hadn't known the meaning of *uxorious*. When he'd looked up the word after the test, he sighed, and spat on page 638 of his *Oxford Desk Dictionary*. He knew he'd never have a wife, anyway. He was sixteen years old and had never kissed a girl. He hadn't tried or wanted to. He'd resigned himself to asexuality early on.

The listeners, even the most rapt ones, will stop the docent at this point, and ask how he knows all these personal details. The docent replies that Zilo IV documented it all in diaries and continues to chronicle his life today. "Zilo IV is only twenty-nine years old, and knowing that he's a part of one of the most important families in American industry, he's quite divulgent for accuracy's sake. On the last day of each month, another detailed diary, swaddled in bubble-wrap and butcher paper, arrives in the museum's mailbox."

Tommy Badde in high school: senior class president, 3.9 GPA in advanced classes, National Honor Society, treasurer of the Young Republicans, varsity tennis and soccer—senior and junior years, first place in Tucson Science Fair for *The Effects of High Vitamin Diets on Chicken Immune Systems* (his grandfather's idea), volunteer at St. Joseph's Soup Kitchen. But sadly, only an 1150 on his SAT.

After history class one morning, the twins stood by their lockers in the crowded hall. Tommy wore a blue-and-gold letter jacket. Zilo IV wore a lawn-green down vest over a black DR. WHO T-shirt. Both boys had the Badde wide-set eyes and dimpled nose tip, only Tommy was tanned from his afternoons on the courts and fields, and worked his face like an exotic supermodel. Zilo IV didn't work his.

"A dollar per point," Zilo IV said flatly. "A dollar for each point, not a dollar for each point by which I improve your pathetic score."

"That's extortion," Tommy said.

"Your misunderstanding of basic words like *extortion* is why you scored a measly 1150."

"You're an asshole, Egg-Boy, and I have a complete understanding of the word *asshole*."

But Tommy wanted more than anything to attend Dartmouth, the Ivy League school farthest from Tucson and his embarrassing family, so he paid his highly intelligent twin brother $1,450 to retake the test for him and raise his score. He was admitted to Dartmouth, and eventually wrote for the hyperconservative *Dartmouth Review.* He penned articles like THREE FRESHMAN WOMEN KILL THEIR UNBORN BABIES, SODOMY CLUB'S MEMBERSHIP DECLINES, and CHECK OUT YOUR MINORITY PROFESSOR — YOU HAVE A RIGHT.

Grandpa was proud of Tommy, and always taped his latest article to the refrigerator in the back room of the egg house. During holiday breaks, Zilo IV ripped down the articles—he didn't care about the politics, he just hated to see Tommy's name in print.

Zilo IV had been flooded with shiny brochures and catalogs from the nation's finest colleges and universities ever since he scored the 1590. In the end, he chose Caltech, where the average SAT score wasn't much lower than his own.

Everyone at Caltech was as brilliant as Zilo. The fat sophomore tuba player who smelled of onions: brilliant. The dreadlocked woman from Manhattan: brilliant. The acne-ravaged basketball player: brilliant. Zilo liked it this way. He learned during the first few days that he could talk to people about particle physics, graphic novels, or endocrinology. He could read, or play on his computer for hours, and no one would pester him. He could walk across the lush Pasadena campus without being shoved or tripped or ridiculed. Other students sat next to him in the cafeteria and spoke to him. They called him by his real name and invited him to parties. And for once, he wasn't smarter than any of his teachers.

When Zilo woke the morning after the first freshman mixer where he had canceled his inhibitions with two warm Millers and danced to German techno music, his face hurt from grinning. He grabbed a pen and his notebook and scrawled the following: *In my four years at Caltech, I will double-major in biochemistry and mechanical engineering with a focus on chicken processing, and I will have sex.* He'd abandoned his plans of a monastic life when he first walked into his dorm and saw the young men and women carrying boxes and stereos and potted plants and bulletin boards and suitcases and trunks. His hall-mates. Both genders. Popcorn pajama parties, all-night cram sessions, intramural coed sports, cheap peeks as they headed to the showers! And they weren't mocking him. Most even smiled. The gamy odor of his hall was what he thought sex might smell like. Each time he walked down it, he breathed deeply, and the stink shot from his nasal membranes to his testicles, making them tingle.

The diploma was something he'd have to wait for. He would read the texts, attend the labs and lectures, take the tests, write the papers and programs, and in four years, he'd graduate with honors and move back to Tucson to revolutionize the chicken farm.

He didn't have to wait too long for the sex.

The docent pauses here, and asks the listeners if he should go on.

Everyone says, "Yes, go on! Go on!"

"The details from the monthly diaries are quite graphic," the docent warns, but the listeners just sit there, mouths slightly agape, and wait for him to elaborate.

Zilo looked in the Yellow Pages, and walked seven blocks to a faded pink cinder-block building: ADULT SHOP. He first noticed the smell inside, like cherry-pie filling. Nothing like his dorm's odor. Then he noticed the bright slickness of it all. Shelves of Silly-Putty–colored dildos, one shaped like a fist. Books. Magazines with titles like *Young Shavers* and *Newcummers*. Mannequins dressed in leather. Inflatable women and men. Wigs on Styrofoam heads.

"Can I help you find something?" the clerk, a skinny, sunburned man, asked Zilo.

"I may need a little time," Zilo said.

"What are you into?"

"I'm not clear on that," Zilo said. "I was hoping something here would pique my interest."

The clerk hefted a large book from a shelf below the dildos. He placed it on the counter. "This book has everything except animals and children." The title, in squishy, bubble-gum letters: VSECHNO. And just below, in smaller, standard typeface, the poor English translation: EVERTHING.

"It's Czech, and it has it all. Penetration shots, and lots of photos of men with women, women with women, men with men. Everything."

Back in his dorm room, with the door locked and the blinds closed, Zilo flipped through his new book. One page featured two men engaged in sex. The English translation read, *Michael receives to buttocks.* A man with an impossibly large penis: *John has spacious bird.* A lesbian love scene: *Zuzan kisses breast-wart of Sally.* All the photos and their captions, even the few Zilo found intriguing, left Zilo amused instead of aroused.

• • •

"So?" the visitors ask the docent. "Did he ever have sex?"

In his material science lab the following week, Zilo noticed a fair-haired ballerino smirking at him as the instructor drew a schematic on the board. Zilo had seen the ballerino before. Todd from Canada. He had performed with celebrated dancers in Europe, and done cancer research in Toronto. He had the face of a mail-away doll: smooth, white, almost shiny, like it had been genetically planned and carefully molded.

As the students filed out of the lab, Todd smirked one last time at Zilo, and haughtily flipped his blond bangs from his eyes. Zilo followed the ballerino as he swaggered back to the dorm.

In the cross-hatched rays of afternoon light that seeped through the closed Venetian blinds, Todd fellated Zilo. The unsummoned gurgles and coos that slipped from Zilo's mouth were surprising and somewhat ridiculous, especially when Zilo found he couldn't control their loudness.

It was over in less than two minutes. When Zilo zipped his trousers, his heart racing away in his chest, he felt like he was forgetting something important. He thanked Todd, kissed his forehead, and mussed his soft hair. Zilo then meandered around campus for a few hours before dinner, wondering.

A few weeks later, he began to have sex with Linda, a woman who lived in a dorm room below his. They'd eat dinner together in the cafeteria, go to their respective rooms for a few hours of study, then Zilo would walk downstairs and knock softly on her door. He enjoyed her giant frizz of red hair, and her large, pillowy breasts. He spent many hours with his head buried in those breasts, while she yawned and stared blankly at the ceiling.

One night, as he kissed her nipples, he muttered, "I love breast warts of you."

"What?"

"It's from a Czech porno book I have. It's a bad translation," Zilo explained. "It's funny."

"Not if you have to explain it." She sighed loudly. "I'm bored. And I'm behind in bio-chem. Maybe we should quit this for a while." She sat up in bed and covered her breasts with a pillow.

Zilo wasn't too upset about the breakup. The same uneasy feeling—like he was forgetting something—had nagged him each time he had messed around with Linda. Sometimes he was left with a hollow feeling in his stomach, almost like the early stages of heartburn.

The rugby player was next. His name was Bradford, and with his buzzed hair and muscular neck, he looked like the guys who had bullied Zilo in high school. Each time Bradford walked near him, Zilo flinched. When

Bradford sat at the same table in the cafeteria, Zilo's throat clenched in fear, and he could no longer swallow his food. This ended one Friday night in November after Zilo had downed his regular three Millers at a dorm party. Bradford busted into the party, flanked by two of his meaty teammates, and handed Zilo a large bottle of Irish beer. Before Zilo had time to get nervous, Bradford leaned down and whispered, "You're just about the cutest."

Zilo woke in Bradford's hairy arms the next morning, bothered again by the nervous hollow in his stomach.

Jill, Dover, Bryce, Bettina, Margie, Courtney, and Ko. Zilo stopped after ten partners: five men and five women, four ethnicities. None of his encounters, even repeated encounters with the same partner, left him feeling good, and that spring, a week before final exams, he made a decision as he pondered his first year at Caltech. He opened his notebook, crossed out *have sex,* and wrote *develop a meaningful (not sexual) relationship.*

He listened to psychologists on the radio and read self-help books. When he met someone new, he no longer thought of sex. Instead, he evaluated his demeanor, her poise, his sense of humor. Could I sit across from this person at the breakfast table and discuss the newspaper? Would this person laugh at my jokes? What kind of a parent would this person be? Does this person like eggs? For the remaining three years at Caltech, Zilo had sex with no one. Each time he had the urge, he'd tick off the questions in his mind, and even if the would-be partner passed the test, he'd remember the hollow feeling in his stomach, and his libido would shrivel.

Zilo refined his chicken-processing ideas during his senior year. He had designed and constructed a de-beaking machine to prevent closely-quartered hens from pecking each other's eyes, performed countless hormone experiments, and, twice per week, drove the twisting freeways to UCLA where he worked with a world-renowned food engineer from Tokyo.

Zilo's family, even Tommy, who had graduated two weeks earlier, traveled to Pasadena for his graduation. They took him out to dinner and toasted his academic achievements.

His grandfather sat next to him, and during the main course of enchiladas, he told him that he couldn't wait for him to start working at the chicken farm. "I looked over the papers you sent me, and I think we can implement all your ideas before the summer's over."

"Great," Zilo said.

"You've got a brain in there like your great-grand-father's," he said, as he knocked on Zilo's head. "You're an inventor and a scientist."

Zilo grinned. The hair on the back of his neck stood in a ticklish way. His ears warmed.

"Hold on there, Grandpa," Tommy said from across the table. "I think my proposal takes precedence over any of Zilo's."

"I've been waiting for your proposal for eight months," Grandpa said. "What could take you so long to propose?"

Tommy cleared his throat and adjusted his tie. "F'neggs," he said proudly.

Often the listener will gasp. "I remember F'neggs! What happened to F'neggs? The Badde family started F'neggs?"

The docent will nod calmly and continue.

"What?" Grandpa said.

"F'neggs. Fun shapes of scrambled eggs for kids of all ages."

"You're joking, right?"

Zilo delighted in his grandfather's incredulity, but as Tommy went on to explain F'neggs—how there were already cold cereals, waffles, and oatmeal for kids, so why not eggs?—and his grandfather nodded and repeated, "Uh-huh," Zilo became bewildered, then frustrated.

Eggy would be the non-gender-specific superhero marketing mascot of F'neggs. The product would be made in four shapes: stars, crescent moons, planets, and rockets. It would be available in four flavors: Ham, Bacon, Nacho, and Plain. Tommy continued to babble, now about marketing strategies, focus groups, and packaging.

"How would the scrambled eggs retain these fun shapes?" Zilo interrupted.

"Ever heard of aspic?" Tommy said.

"And why the space theme?"

"Eggy's from outer space, Zilo," Tommy snapped. "Try listening."

"I think this Eggy character is wonderful," Grandpa said. "I think F'neggs are wonderful!"

Everyone at the table clapped for Tommy, except Zilo, who rolled his eyes, then asked, "How much per unit? I'm assuming each of these F'neggs will be three ounces."

"I haven't determined that," Tommy said.

Zilo did some quick calculations in his head. He saw compounds forming. He followed hormones as they coursed through a hen's system. "If you really want to develop this absurd idea, I can guarantee a three-ounce unit for under seven cents—any of the flavors, any of the shapes. In fact, through intravenous feeding and hormonal manipulation, the hens will produce preflavored eggs that will hold their fun shapes without adding gelatin." He thought for a few seconds more, and then promised that the eggs would even contain morsels that resembled ham chunks, bacon bits, or nacho cheese balls.

"To our Zilo!" Grandpa toasted, raising his glass with one hand, and gripping Zilo's shoulder with the other.

"Remember," Tommy said, "F'neggs were my idea."

The docent becomes silent, closes his eyes tightly, and grips the edge of his desk. His lips move quickly, but he says nothing the visitors can hear. *Dark Cornish are crossbred with Araucana. The resultant pullets are used in the F'neggs Project. At nine weeks, pullets are deposited headfirst into Prep-Machine #3, beak aligned with red arrow on the front of the depository. They are de-beaked, and the consequent laceration, "beak hole," is sprayed with 15 ml of 10 M Sulfacetamide solution, and daubed with .85 g Neomycin/Polymycin B Sulfates ointment . . .*

The docent shudders, then proceeds with the history.

In November, the first F'neggs were produced. After government approval, they were test-marketed in Kansas City, Mobile, and Baltimore. Zilo and Tommy spent hours reading returned questionnaires. Common queries and criticisms: *Why are the ham chunks blue?* or *The nacho balls are gritty* or *Eggy is dumb.* Nothing serious. No allergic reactions or other medical problems, no complaints of utter disgust.

After Zilo adjusted the ham and nacho cheese hens' diets, F'neggs hit the freezers of supermarkets across the country. The Eggy commercials ran on the three major networks, once per thirty minutes every Saturday morning, and all week on Nickelodeon and MTV. Demand was higher than projected. Kids clamored for Eggy merchandise, wrote letters addressed to Eggy, called the Badde Chicken Farm, and www.fneggs.com was often impossible to access because of heavy traffic. Most supermarkets had to start F'neggs waiting lists to avoid the mobs on days when shipments arrived. Ricky Martin and Cher were photographed buying F'neggs. Articles about Tommy and Zilo ran in influential business magazines. The Badde Chicken Farm halted all production other than F'neggs. Several more Prep-Machines were constructed, and millions of pullets were prepped. Oscar Mayer, Louis Rich, and Frank Perdue each tried to copy F'neggs, but their products never held their shapes, and their flavors like *Pizza Party, Hot-Dawg,* and *Buttery* were flops. The kids wanted the real thing: F'neggs, each box featuring the smiling cartoon Eggy riding a rocket through outer space, each unit holding its shape better than a kitchen sponge.

Zilo developed a crush on a Pullet Depositor named Gina. He watched her working in the factory from his laboratory upstairs. She stuffed each of the squirming, squawking pullets into Prep-Machine #3F with care, her tongue sticking out a little in concentration. Colorful plastic barrettes held her long white hair out of her face, and every time Zilo walked by, she was humming old disco tunes. Zilo liked her calm nature, how her serene expression never changed. He liked her juvenile hairstyle. Watching her helped him forget his work, the tiresome hours in the lab under fluorescent lights, injecting hens and concocting additives.

Zilo remained true to the promise he had made to himself years earlier: *Try to develop a meaningful (not sexual) relationship.* He asked Gina out on dates where they'd be surrounded by people. He took her on picnics in crowded parks, to movies, to museums. Whenever they were alone, he'd make up an excuse and leave.

She called him after six dates. "What gives?" she asked. "We've been out a lot, and we haven't even held hands."

"I don't want to rush into anything," Zilo said.

"Is it because I work for you?" Gina said. "I'm not one of those sue-happy sexual harassment sluts, if that's what you're worried about."

"I don't want to feel hollow," Zilo said.

"What?"

"When I rush into relationships, I end up feeling hollow."

"I've started to date Vince, the Placer in Coop Seven," Gina said. "How does that make you feel?"

"Bad," Zilo said, "but not hollow."

That evening, as he handed a twenty-dollar bill to an aged hustler kneeling before him in the pungent oleanders on the north side of Himmel Park, he said, "Now I feel hollow."

And later in the week, after he had sex with a sun-ravaged prostitute in a dusty South Sixth Avenue motel room, he said to her, "Yup, hollow. Definitely hollow. You know what I mean?"

She smoothed her stockings and fixed her makeup in the mirror. "If you want me to say *yes,* I'll say *yes,*" she mumbled impassively. "If you want me to say *no,* I'll say *no.*"

At work, he found himself watching Gina more often, wondering if he was doomed to alternate between polysexual fuck monster—the actual term Zilo used to describe himself in his diary—and sexless monk. Would he ever find someone patient enough to abide his socio-psycho-sexual dysfunction? Probably not. So he focused on work like never before.

"Poor guy," the museum visitors say. "He could have made it work with Gina. He's not a polysexual fuck monster, he's just confu—"

"Zilo is a smart man," the docent interrupts, "but

even he couldn't have predicted what happened next."

The first rumor was this: A nine-year-old girl in Seattle who had eaten Ham F'neggs as a midnight snack died. Her mother shook her shoulder to wake her for school, and her head collapsed like a rotten jack-o'-lantern, spewing gray, chunky liquid over her pillow. Next, an illustrated letter to the *Boston Globe* revealed the similarity between the F'neggs logo on Eggy's chest—an egg surrounded by seven stars—to an ancient Wiccan symbol meaning "family death." F'neggs were pulled from the shelves in the South. Schoolchildren gossiped that Cher was losing her hair because of F'neggs, and that F'neggs made Ricky Martin gay. Kids everywhere stopped eating F'neggs. Parents and celebrities stopped buying them.

The Baddes responded by changing the logo on Eggy's chest to a smiling planet, and adding two new flavors: *Arizona Ranch* and *Texas Barbecue*. Nothing worked, though, and the profits plummeted as quickly as they had skyrocketed.

Tommy began to hound Zilo in the lab. He yelled, "Think! Think of something new!" Tommy paced the halls above the egg house, began to wear the same oil-stained white dress shirt and khakis every day. He didn't shave. His hair became matted and he began to smell foul. Gone were his robust Ivy League countenance and cocky swagger.

Zilo ignored Tommy for those next months and quietly went about his work, refining the de-beaking antibiotics and the feeding-tube-insertion procedure. He worked, too, on breeding beakless blind hens that could never peck at anything, only lay eggs, maybe even shell-free eggs, eggs that would plop into systems of aluminum gutters. He envisioned huge vats of swirling yolk—no useless shells. Zilo knew he was close to achieving all this the afternoon his grandfather walked into the lab.

"We need to talk," his grandfather said. "We're closing up shop."

"I'm just about there," Zilo said. "I'm close to cutting the unit price to less than three cents."

"Tommy's lost his mind."

"Tommy's always been superfluous," Zilo said. "One twin always is."

"Clean out your bank accounts, because we're through," Grandpa said. "We're bankrupt. The world hates F'neggs. They hate Eggy. They hate us."

The docent stops. He refuses to go on, even if the listeners beg—which they often do. "I can't," the docent says. "I'm terribly sorry." He thanks them as they leave,

sighs when none of them drops money into the DONA-
TIONS bucket.

In the early evenings, the docent doffs his dark glasses,
placing them in his top desk drawer. On his way home,
he walks by the former button factory and winces as he
breathes in the thick tire fumes. He kicks through the
wet grass along the Mississippi, stops to collect old
shells with button blanks cut from them. Through the
holes in the shells, he gazes at the sparkling water, at the
tall river oaks on the Illinois side, at the birds pecking
through the soft earth in the dying light. The docent
rarely sees another person along the river, but he keeps
looking, hoping he'll find someone who won't make
him feel hollow.

Worms

The pretty lady reporter had quickly introduced herself as Dora Hawkins, and right away began to interview Billy Hair about his worm farm, scribbling notes, flipping through her pad, all the while struggling to save her shoes from the mud. Despite her appearance—a delicate beauty only pampering could produce—Dora Hawkins was nothing like the Dallas belles Billy had served at his aunt's café during his humdrum youth. Those girls were reared to accept, even expect, a life of indulgence and repose. They would drive up to Olney with their daddies on oil-scouting trips, and they'd inevitably stop at the café, the town's only restaurant, where they'd roll their eyes and sigh before complaining about the food and the unsanitary conditions. They scared Billy. They were rich, unapproachable, and mean. Once a belle griped about Billy specifically: "Daddy, ask if there's someone besides this chip-toothed redneck who can attend to us." Her hair was sprayed up tall, and the loose, gold bracelet that dangled from her wrist clanged against her soup bowl. Her daddy did ask, and Billy's aunt said there wasn't anyone else, but that Billy would stretch his lip over his tooth. Billy had wasted so many years in the café, staring out at the dusty fields.

Sometimes the memories of the café returned with such immediacy that he jumped, thinking he could actually hear the sizzle of the grill, or smell the chicken-fried steaks, or see the snobbishness in customers' eyes.

Dora Hawkins gripped her pen tightly as she scratched in her pad. The blue veins on her precious hands emerged like worms during a steamy June downpour. Billy could see her conviction. She wasn't lazy; she wasn't stuck on herself. And this made him think too far ahead. Dora Hawkins had walked onto his farm only minutes earlier, and already he was wondering what it would be like if she were his wife.

But Dora's professors had not taught her to snare a husband, just as they had not taught her to luxuriate and let her brain atrophy. They imparted instead a drive to succeed, a fervor to struggle for what she believed was right. With her education, she could change the world! By her last year of college, she had decided on a career: journalism. She'd start as a print reporter, then move on to television, where she'd not only chase stories but anchor the newscast. She would. Her professors had told her that if she set her mind to it and worked diligently, she could.

Yet the world outside the small, safe haven of school was different: more formidable, less accommodating. The fast-talking newspapermen in Manhattan scoffed at her résumé —three years on the staff of the *Weekly Vassar*—so she traveled south to Raleigh, where the newsmen said they'd never heard of Vassar College or its Yankee paper. Next she boarded a train for Dallas. The fat men in their ill-fitting trousers and spit-shined cowboy boots called her a "pretty little honey" and laughed when she handed them a folder of clippings. "We could use you in the secretary pool if you can type," one said, eyes locked on her breasts. On her way out of the sweaty office, feeling defrauded by her professors and defeated by the chauvinists, ready to head home to her parents in Connecticut, she met a secretary who tugged at her sleeve, guided her into a supply closet. "They need a reporter in Wichita," the woman whispered. "My sister's a reporter there. Wichita's small, but nice."

"Kansas?"

"No, honey. Wichita Falls, Texas. Up near Oklahoma, about three hours by car."

Ford Fordrusher, editor in chief of the *Wichita Falls Journal,* hired Dora minutes after meeting her. "I don't know about your college, but you know your pronouns."

"Thank you," Dora said, puzzled.

Ford didn't call her *honey* or *darlin,* didn't stare at her breasts. He combed his gray hair like her father did, a perfect part just above his left ear. "You'll do some copyediting, and some reporting of your own," he said. "We have to dig for news around here, but we put out a good read."

A week later, Dora's smart oxford shoes—shoes neither too masculine nor too feminine—were coated in heavy mud. She was in Olney, interviewing Billy Hair. About worming. A heavy stench of manure and rot. Vast fields of brown, browner than the rest of this brown part of Texas.

"I've been worming since my aunt died seven years ago," Billy told Dora, still marveling at her as she stood in the brutal July sun. He wondered if she'd ever suffered sunburn or a blister. Had she ever fallen off a pony and scraped her elbow? Even in this pressing heat, her skin was like the film on cream in the morning, delicate and white. "She left me the café, which I closed and leveled right away, and all this land, which was mostly dust." He should offer to buy her new shoes, he thought. Maybe he could drive her down to Dallas to find real nice ones. They could eat lunch at a restaurant with tablecloths and linen napkins. The sun would sink as they drove home, and the wide Texas sky would be lit in brilliant blends of pink and orange. They'd pull over and kiss in the last of the day's light. "I was the first to breed brandling manure worms with deep-burrowing worms," he added.

"I'm utterly unfamiliar with worms, Mr. Hair," Dora said. "They didn't give me time to research. I'm sorry."

"I'll teach you," he said, smiling, exposing that chipped tooth. "Brandlings do their business below-ground. Worm waste is where the nutrients are at. The deep-burrowing worms lay their waste above. What we needed was a worm who'd shit deep under the dirt, near the tips of the roots." He pointed to himself. "I made them. Sorry about saying 'shit.' "

"Not a problem," Dora said, flipping the pages of her pad. "Most of these hybrids go to farmers?"

"Yes," Billy said. "Treat the worms nice, and they'll reward you ten times over."

"I see." Dora looked at Billy, who still grinned. He was stout, a little husky. A few black curls peeked from under his sweat-soaked cap. "And this is the only worm farm in North Texas?"

"Only one this size west of the Mississippi, Miss Dora."

She liked the way he stood, legs apart, rocking on the heels of his tall boots. Like he was ready for something to happen. If he called her "Miss Dora" again, she'd smile back. "So farmers can grow crops without soil additives, without topsoil destruction?" she asked.

"That's right. And the same worms, because they're redder than most and wiggle real good, make the best hooking worms." He removed his cap, ran thick fingers through his damp curls. "You fish?"

"I have," Dora said proudly. "My father took me all the way to Montana once. Fly-fishing."

"I can't picture a pretty lady like you out there in waders, Miss Dora."

She smiled, noticed a thin, horizontal scar on his chin, maybe an inch long. No whiskers grew along the scar, a pink stripe among greenish stubble. Barroom brawl? Farming accident? Rodeo mishap? Maybe he had defended his mother, or a homely sister. "I've fished on lakes and ponds, too," she said. "I've baited my own hooks."

"Did you now?"

"I did," Dora said. "Once I caught a catfish as big as your arm."

This reciprocal attention scared Billy a little, made

his stomach twitch like it hadn't twitched in years, caused his throat to bunch up. "I'd love to talk fishing with you, Miss Dora, but I got to get back to work." He pointed westward, into the brown. "I'm fixin' to flood three fields today."

His hand was rough and heavy, but when they shook he gripped hers gingerly, as if his real hand— gentle, careful, that of a surgeon or symphony conductor—was trapped inside an armor of calluses and dirt. Dora took a chance. She asked where she could fish around here.

"You didn't see the signs for Lake Arrowhead?" Billy asked.

That Saturday, Dora met Billy at the lake. He didn't pick her up at home because he didn't know Wichita Falls, didn't want to. Each time he went up there a new supermarket or auto dealership had appeared, throwing off his sense of direction. He preferred to buy his groceries in Olney and his trucks in Archer City. He'd have never found Dora's apartment; he would likely have driven the wrong way on one of the twisting new freeways and ended up in Iowa Park or Burkburnett.

Dora wore pressed Levi's and one of her father's white Brooks Brothers button-downs. Billy wore his old dungarees and a white snap shirt. Each realized they were dressed alike, but neither said anything. Both thought it was a good omen.

On the boat, in the middle of the brown, still lake, Dora told Billy his hands were beautiful, that they evinced hard work, which she admired. "Not many people work hard these days," she said. "Not as hard as you."

"I spent yesterday reading a comic while my fields flooded," he said. "Yogi Bear."

"I bet." Then, remembering her inspiring professors—especially sad Dr. Farr, who had tearfully confessed on the last day of class that she had hidden in academia because she was afraid to love—Dora lightly kissed Billy's hand and held it to her flushed cheek. He felt her tiny earlobe with his big fingers.

The boat rocked a little. The sun emerged from the clouds, and the lake's brown tint drained to blue. "How did you get that scar?" she asked.

"My older brother."

"And the chipped tooth?"

"Same day," Billy said. "Same shove."

Billy changed the subject to fish he had caught. He rarely spoke of the day his tooth was chipped and his chin scarred. He'd been seven when it happened. In the station wagon with his parents and his brother, Shane, on their way to Fat McBride's Steakhouse in Wichita Falls for Sunday supper. Billy's mother always warned him to pee before they got in the car, but that day he'd been out back practicing with the lasso and lost track of time. Shane had taught him how to throw the rope from his hip so as not to startle the horse, and Billy had worked all afternoon, straining his wrist, blistering his palms.

"Please pull over, Daddy," Billy said from the back-seat as the car topped Chalk Hill.

"Billy didn't pee at home," Shane said.

"I forgot," Billy said. "I have to go real bad."

"Maybe if you held it until McBride's, you wouldn't forget next time," his father said, slowing and pulling onto the shoulder. Billy felt the reassuring crackle of gravel and dirt under the tires. He swung open the door, stood in its shadow just outside the car, and fumbled with the buttons of his jeans.

He didn't recall hearing anything, just remembered feeling his brother's hard shove. Flat on his face, metallic taste of blood, burrs and pebbles sticking in his weenie, and the deafening squeal and boom of the hay truck taking out the station wagon and his family. When Billy looked up from the ground and saw the mess—his mother and daddy strewn on the asphalt like rags, Shane lost in the mashed car, glowing bits of hay floating in the sunlight like millions of tiny angels—he sprinted into the range that flanked the highway, scattering the cattle with his wails. He fell sideways into a dry ravine and slept, clutching his lasso-sore forearm to his chest. Distorted, intense images of twirling ropes and runaway horses filled his dreams.

The September wedding was held in Connecticut, a spectacle for Dora's family and friends. She was marrying an uneducated Texan of ambiguous ancestry who spoke of using earthworms to revolutionize agriculture.

Billy had no close kin, and the few relatives he'd told about the wedding couldn't afford to attend. Dora didn't pry. She knew how Billy had lost his parents and brother. A few months after that first date, she looked up the story on microfilm in the paper's archive room, spent two hours in the dusty darkness before the headline slid onto the screen: FOUR DIE IN CHALK HILL COLLISION. Once she read it, she wished she hadn't; she felt awful for Billy, pictured him as a boy, orphaned, living with the aunt who forced him to work in that shabby café. She felt bad that Billy hadn't told her himself, felt it in her gut. And when he finally did confide in her, the night he proposed marriage, she knew he loved her completely.

At first Dora's parents thought she had chosen Billy in retaliation against the orderly life they had laid out for her. She had rebelled once before, during her final year at Miss Porter's, attaching herself to her horsy beret-and-turtleneck-wearing roommate, Brenda, and bringing her home for the holidays (during which time they were always hand in hand, even at the dinner table), then insisting on touring Europe with her after graduation. Thank God Dora had the smarts to leave Brenda in Lisbon and return home a month early, saying, "If either of you ever utters the name 'Brenda,' I swear, I will never speak to you again!" Her parents were relieved when young men from Wesleyan and Yale, even disheveled bohemian types with straggly goatees and frayed corduroys, called for Dora during breaks from college.

But this Billy Hair!

"It was an accident," Billy told Dora's mother a few days prior to the nuptials. "A wonderful accident."

"Oh," Dora's mother said impassively, sitting stiffly in a chair that looked neither comfortable nor sturdy. She nibbled a biscuit and sipped her tea without altering her posture.

"I left the flood pipes on too long, and water got into the manure pasture. Next thing I know, I see the diggers and the manure worms tangling with one another!" His eyes widened. "At first I thought they were fightin', like for territory, but then I saw the sexual mucus, and I knew they were fixin' to mate."

"Sexual mucus?" Dora's mother dropped the biscuit.

It missed her tiny plate and crumbled on the floor. "I'm sure I'm unfamiliar with sexual mucus."

"The important thing is that the worms, two types of worms, were in a matin' frenzy. It was like they'd been waitin' years to get with each other."

"Does Dora know all this?"

"She wrote up a nice article for the Wichita paper about it. That's how we met."

"Oh, yes," Dora's mother said, "I remember her mentioning that."

Dora's father collared Billy in the evening, in the den. "So, Mr. Hair," he said, scanning the bookshelves on his wall, touching the bindings with his middle finger like he was counting them, "what kind of name is 'Hair'?"

"Mine," Billy said, glancing up from a golf magazine. "My daddy's first."

"Yes," Mr. Hawkins said, "but what about genealogy? Where did your ancestors live?"

"Mostly in Throckmorton," Billy said, "though some on my mother's side had dairy farms outside Windthorst."

"That's not what I mean."

"I know what you mean, sir." Billy felt the way he had as a kid, serving Dallas debutantes in the café. He looked down at the magazine in his lap: a man in knickers and argyle socks, bent at the waist, ready to putt. He could hear Mr. Hawkins breathing fiercely through his nostrils. It made Billy feel extra lucky that Dora was sweet on him, just a wormer with dirt under his nails.

Billy and Dora honeymooned on Lake Winnipesaukee in New Hampshire. They stayed in Dora's uncle's cabin, a small place with log walls and a stone fireplace. A path of slate slabs led to the shore, another to the woods, where Billy dug his fingers and elbows into the moist dirt—never had felt soil like it. Dora gazed up into the trees, breathed in the smells. They made noises they never had before, grunted even, and moved their bodies in new ways. They spent hours in the forest discovering each other, both lost in waves of giddy urgency.

They skinny-dipped at night, their white bodies catching moonbeams in the chilly black water. Fish brushed Billy's legs, and weeds tangled in his toes, reminding him where he was, who he was with, that this was really happening. Dora was his wife. He was her husband. They would be together forever.

Billy's face ached from grinning when he woke that first morning. He could have stayed in that musty bed for days, stroking those soft arms. And Dora would have been content to remain there, too—as long as she could make him smile and see the adorable chipped tooth. As long as his eyes still widened when he talked of his worms. Who was it, she wondered, who said true beauty exists only in the imperfect? Maybe she had said it.

But both knew they must return to Texas, Dora to finish a story on Klan activity in Bowie, Billy to begin his new worm work in earnest. He had bought several ten-pound bags of egg capsules from a man in Tennessee. These capsules held young burrowing worms that would grow to ten or twelve inches. Billy speculated that a good crossbreeding with his brand-lings would yield worms perfect for the Christmas-tree farmers up north, who needed hardy worms that would commit to a single root mass for five or six years. They'd be matchless for tuber farming, too, indulging those potatoes and yams big-time. And no topsoil erosion. His new spring-tooth harrow and tractor would allow him to feed his worms faster than ever, to roll over the mud without getting stuck. Flood two hundred more acres, solicit more supermarkets and farmers for old produce, more horse breeders and cattlemen for manure. Maybe hire some employees, build a worming empire.

Billy's modern equipment proved as useful as he had hoped; the egg-capsule harvests that fall and winter were his best yet. With Dora's help placing ads in rural newspapers, he sold his new hybrids to over forty potato farmers in one Idaho county alone. The Dallas paper ran an article about him in the business section, and soon editors from agricultural journals all over the country were calling.

Dora's investigative reporting for the *Journal* never seemed to pick up after the wedding. The Klan article flopped. The only incident in the area had transpired at Bowie Junior High, where three white boys had forced a black boy to wear a dress. "We don't hate Gerry 'cause he's a Negro," one of the perpetrators told Dora, "we hate him because he tries to kiss us at lunch." No signs of organized Klan activity. Another dead end. She was tired of making stinks about nothing: RACIAL TENSION ERUPTS IN BOWIE SCHOOL SYSTEM.

Then there was the series on the drug trade. She never beat the reporters from Dallas and Fort Worth to the hot leads, so her articles felt stale. ROUGHNECK AMPHETAMINE USE ON THE RISE — BUT YOU ALREADY KNEW THAT BECAUSE IT WAS IN THE DALLAS PAPERS LAST WEEK.

Dora knew her best stories were profiles of locals, like the one she had written about Billy. She drove out to Mineral Wells to interview an old woman who lived in a house made of bottles, and her story elicited over fifty flattering letters—the most ever for a profile in the *Journal,* Ford Fordrusher said. For the next few years she hunted down oddball human-interest stories. In Jacksboro, twin champion bull riders married twin champion baton-twirlers. In Holliday, a woman sold her catfish pie recipe to a French chef for five hundred dollars. Near Scotland, a weathered geezer collected skunk pelts along Highway 25 and sewed a teepee in which he lived all winter.

But the profiles didn't satisfy Dora. There was no necessity about them. Ford set few deadlines. They filled space; they weren't news. But then, after nearly forty stories, an editor from *Life* magazine called. "My brother lives in Wichita Falls," he told her. "He sends me good stuff from local papers. I've shown your clippings around the offices here in New York. We admire your work."

"Thank you." Her face burned with glee.

"If you could augment the piece about the nuns' goat farm, I think we'd buy it. We also like the one about the rodeo clown. . . ."

Dora ran into the swampy field to tell Billy, her boots sucking and collecting mud, sinking dangerously deep every fifth step or so. Heavier and heavier. Her thighs ached. The sun hung in the late-day haze—an orange disk, not tough to look at, especially because it held Billy's silhouette.

Billy was riding his noisy feeding tractor, so Dora bent and scooped a blob of mud and chunked it at him to get his attention, hitting the back of his head. He switched off the thrumming engine. "What the hell?"

he said, wiping his neck with a bandana. When he turned and saw Dora, he grinned.

"*Life!*" she yelled. She climbed aboard the tractor and sat on Billy's lap, muddying his dungarees. "*Life.* They want some of my profiles."

"That's great," he said, confused.

"I'm not even telling my parents," she said. "Let them hear about it from someone else."

Dora's contributor note for the magazine read, *Dora Hawkins writes for the* Wichita Falls Journal *and lives with her husband on an experimental farm in Texas.*

"Got your name wrong," Billy said, reading at the kitchen table. "Used your old one."

"The editor I worked with thought 'Hair' was odd-sounding," Dora said from the den. "He said it might distract readers." She walked into the kitchen and stood above Billy, noticed for the first time his curls were thinning. Slick scalp was barely visible on the crown of his head.

"Your story sure looks nice," Billy said. He flipped through the bright photographs of nuns with goats; one sister was wearing a habit, bottle-feeding a kid. "You hate your name? You hate Hair?"

"Of course not," Dora said.

"Your daddy doesn't like it."

"But I love it." It wasn't the lie that concerned her; it

was the ease with which it had spilled from her lips, like liquid.

Billy was nearly incapacitated with guilt when Dora began to retch early each morning. Just as the sun boiled over the brown flatness, she'd hop out of bed and race to the toilet. Some afternoons Billy would be on his tractor, thinking of pregnant Dora, and he'd forget why he was out there, where he was headed. Once he nearly drove into the pond. When Dora began to show, he felt worse. He'd rarely leave her side, hated it when she drove off to Wichita in the late morning. He had done this to her; her back ached, and she suffered through hemorrhoids and nausea, all because of him. He had put that baby in there. Dora let him feel her stomach when the baby kicked, and the slight fluttery movements startled him.

He wanted that child out of there.

Blackness circled Dora's eyes. Her breasts filled and looked different, like those of women on calendars at gas stations—rounder, heavier. Billy felt dirty when he admired them, like he was admiring another woman's breasts.

No more sex: from the first morning when Dora told him she was pregnant, he never entertained the idea.

No way. Not with that baby in there. Not with Dora looking—and sometimes acting—like a stranger. Dora thought about sex, though, more than ever. But the things she tried in bed scared Billy, especially during the third trimester, when she looked as if she could pop.

"Don't be touching me there," Billy said, grabbing her wrist. "I told you."

"I thought maybe since you had those beers with dinner," Dora said, rolling onto her back, resting her hands on her distended abdomen.

"Please don't touch me like that until after the baby's born. You'll make me crazy."

Soon he snored. Dora lay awake, drummed her fingers on her stomach, and thought of the days when Billy would trudge in from the fields wet with sweat and stinky with mud. He'd kiss her in the kitchen until she insisted he take a bath, and she'd join him.

Now she didn't even like the way she fit in the tub. Displaced too much water.

A girl. Hair dark and curly as Billy's, skin pink like Dora's when she used to blush. Tiny hands, dimpled, and gripping nothing. Billy felt relief like never before. With the baby safely bundled in the nursery, he climbed onto the hospital bed with Dora and fell into a deep slumber, his head on her shoulder. Dora didn't sleep at first, couldn't; the scent of the farm in Billy's hair wouldn't let her. It was wrong to smell that smell in the clean, white, antiseptic hospital. Besides, they needed a name. Billy had refused to discuss it, said it was bad luck to name a child before it came out. He snored lightly, slowly. How could he breathe that slowly? She turned her head, stretched the sheet over her mouth and nose—a filter—and finally fell asleep.

Because of the new baby, Dora wrote fewer articles. Ford Fordrusher had insisted she slow down, and *Life* wouldn't buy another from her region until next year. Still, she headed to the office each afternoon, just for two or three hours, enough time to miss her newborn: Charlotte, named for Billy's cousin and Dora's great-aunt, the only girls' name the Hairs and Hawkinses shared.

Meanwhile, Billy was left at home with the baby. The diapers and feedings were no problem. He sat in his mother's old chair and rocked away the hours, humming to Charlotte, tickling her chin, making her smile. But as much as he loved his new daughter—and later he would remember how much, remind himself how much—these afternoons with her bored him. He'd look over his land and itch with frustration, thinking of the fields he should flood, the hybrids he should test, the compost he should spread. His newest tractor sat dormant just outside. It shone red, like candy.

He knew he should cherish these days. Charlotte wouldn't be a baby forever. A few teeth had already sprouted from her tiny gums, sharp things that cut through rubber nipples every few days, making her gurgle and choke on the warm formula. Her eyes were big, a shade of blue so bright they seemed unnatural. And she'd look up at Billy from the end of her bottle like she sensed his boredom, like she knew he'd rather be tromping around outside, playing with his worms.

During Charlotte's fourth-birthday party, a neighbor girl told Billy that Charlotte had called her a "retard." Dora once caught her daughter taping a note to the mailbox, presumably for the letter carrier: YUO ARE UGLE. Then there was the day when Billy watched as Charlotte threw potatoes she had stolen from the kitchen at the old, blind barn cat. She laughed as she scared the feeble creature from its restful perch on the tractor seat. When she ambushed Dora, hiding behind the couch and smacking her in the shins with a big book of fairy tales, Dora sat Billy down for a talk.

"She's bored is all," he said. "We need to take her somewhere besides this worm farm."

"Not all farm kids act like her," Dora said. "There are plenty of good doctors in Dallas."

"I'll take her to Wichita Falls tomorrow. Just me and her. I'll talk to her in the truck."

They'd go first to the department store, where Charlotte could choose her own dress. Next they'd drive to the photographer to have her portrait taken for inclusion with the Christmas greetings. If all went well, Billy would take her out for ice cream, maybe a sundae. Then they'd return home and ride the tractor to the pond, where Bruce, Charlotte's surly goose, lived. She would feed Bruce the bread heels she had collected during the week. Just Daddy and Daddy's little girl.

Now Billy stood above his daughter on the sidewalk in front of the ice-cream parlor. Charlotte was on her hands and knees, slapping a puddle of pink vomit, vomit she forced up when Billy told her she was not getting ice cream because of her behavior at the photographer's studio. "Look what you made me do!" she screamed.

Billy fantasized about running to his truck and driving away, his tires spinning and squealing, drowning out his daughter's screams. He'd get arrested. His photo would be on the front page of the paper where his wife worked, the one he read every morning. The photo would be clear; Dora would make sure. The headline would read: FATHER ABANDONS DAUGHTER IN PARKING LOT.

His scenario continued: Charlotte running after his

truck, panicked. Maybe she'd trip, skin both her knees . . . and her hands. She'd vomit again. It was bad to think this, he knew, but he couldn't stop—the thoughts unraveled like colorful ribbons. Some poor sucker would help little Charlotte, hug her, ask where her mommy was. Charlotte would tell the sucker that he or she was fat or ugly or retarded and to stop touching her.

"Please get up," Billy told Charlotte. "Please."

"No!" She slapped the vomit again. "No!"

A few droplets dotted Billy's boots. "If you want to play in your mess all day, be my guest."

"I hate you," she said.

"I don't hate you," he said, hoping he wasn't lying. "Get up, please."

She stood, wiped her hands and mouth on her dress. Without looking at her father, she marched to his truck and stood there until he opened the door for her. She climbed in and snapped the seat belt over her waist.

Fifty miles of brown silence with Charlotte seated as far away as possible, her face pressed against the dusty window. He forgot to slow down the way he always did at Chalk Hill, forgot to whisper the prayers to his parents and brother. When he realized this later in bed, the thoughts of abandoning Charlotte in the parking lot surfaced again.

Dora took two weeks off to tackle her daughter's problems. She bought paint kits and crayons, and between tantrums and crying sessions Charlotte created masterpieces: a detailed portrait of Bruce, her goose; a landscape of trees and mountains; a bowl of fruit. No sticks and blobs, no smiling sun in the corner, no copied cartoons. These were real works with perspective, with balance.

The specialists in Dallas deemed Charlotte emotionally normal, not antisocial, not neurotic. They could only confirm what Dora and Billy already knew: She was a precocious, highly intelligent, artistic, and ill-natured four-year-old. "Sometimes," one psychologist told Dora, "children with verbal aptitudes as prematurely developed as Charlotte's know they can deeply affect or hurt people with their words. She's just testing her skills, her new power."

"Did you tell them she called me a 'turd'?" Billy asked one night.

"I tell them everything," Dora said. "Can't we just take a bath?" She unbuttoned her blouse, stood in the yellow light of the bathroom, wanted Billy to shut up and undress. He could scrub her back with the boar's-hair brush and massage her temples. She turned on the water, spoke louder. "We just have to nod through this for a while."

"How long?" Billy asked.

"I don't know. The doctors don't know. No one knows."

"Make up something," Billy said. "Make up a date so I have something to look forward to."

"She starts kindergarten in nine months."

"Nine months," Billy said. "Like a pregnancy."

The day after Christmas, Billy sat in the den in his mother's old rocking chair, reading agricultural periodicals. He always looked for his own advertisements, the ones Dora had written and placed:

BILLY HAIR'S WORMS

HYBRIDS FOR ANY CROP

EGG CAPSULES SENT VIA U.S. MAIL

He liked seeing his name in print. It was childish, he knew, but it made him feel important.

Charlotte sat at his feet, playing with her new toys: a wooden train set, plastic circus animals, a few picture books, a battery-operated doll that crawled. She had been good for the last few weeks, well-behaved and pleasant for a four-year-old—any four-year-old. She hadn't said anything rude; there had been no incidents since her last visit to the doctors in Dallas. In fact, she demonstrated a new fondness for her daddy, often crawled into Billy's lap and let him read to her. She pointed out words she knew.

"You smell like mud," she whispered to Billy today, sitting sidesaddle on his leg, looking at his farming journal.

"Sorry," he said. "I haven't had a chance to shower."

"It's good," she said. She pressed her nose into his neck and sniffed. "It's Christmas mud smell."

"This magazine's no fun for you. Pick one of your new books from the floor."

"I'll play with my doll now," she said, climbing down.

For Christmas, Charlotte had given her parents paintings, her best works yet. To Dora, a portrait of Billy—chin scar, chipped tooth, and all. In the portrait, his hair was combed back and he wore a dotted tie. Dora hadn't seen him in a tie since their wedding. For Billy, Charlotte painted a diagram of a worm, copied from one of his books, only livened up; she had carefully considered how the light played off the moist crinkles and folds, and the effect, when Billy squinted a little, was nearly photographic.

In a while they'd bundle up, and Billy would take Charlotte across the muddy field on his tractor. Charlotte would feed Bruce some leftover stuffing from Christmas dinner. Billy would avoid the spitting goose, and sample the earth from the pond's soft shore, test its nitrate level. Dora would be back from Wichita Falls when they returned, and supper—maybe just turkey sandwiches and rewarmed potatoes—would be on the table. For now, Charlotte was content with her doll, and Billy with his article on corn roots. The space heater hissed and gurgled.

Dora found Billy asleep in the chair, his mouth open, a line of drool working its way down his scar. She kissed him awake. He didn't jerk, just opened his eyes and smiled. She dug through the papers in her bag, the late-afternoon light pouring through the window, infusing her hair, making it shine like black liquid. He wiped his flannel sleeve across his chin.

"Where's Charlotte?" Dora asked, looking up.

"Maybe in her room," Billy said, but he was already pulling on his boots, grabbing his coat.

He stood on the porch a moment, scanning the horizon, which glistened with the last rays of sun. Looked out toward the pond. He raced to his tractor and roared off, not hearing Dora's cries for her daughter.

As he neared the pond, Billy saw Charlotte. His little girl bobbed lightly toward the edge, her arms the blue-white of a catfish belly, her swaying black curls shrouding her head. She was still clutching a plastic bread sack of crumbs and leftovers. He knew instantly what had happened. She had stepped too close, hadn't stayed in the weedy area where the ground was solid, and she'd tripped, was sucked in, her legs caught in the mucky bottom. Billy and Dora had warned her over and over about the mud fields, about getting stuck, but they didn't think to warn her about the pond, never thought she'd walk all the way there by herself. She'd never even tried before, had always asked for a ride on the tractor. Billy envisioned his daughter trying to wake him, then collecting the crumbs and heading out.

Bruce paddled alongside Charlotte, honking territorially as Billy hurried into the water. The pond was only waist deep, but the mud at the bottom was thicker and colder than he had imagined. He kicked around for a rock or a stump to stand on. When he finally grabbed Charlotte's lifeless arm, Bruce pecked at his wrist, at his head. Honked and spat and bit and stirred up from the water. Before Billy was able to grab a fistful of oily feathers, his ear was bleeding. The warm blood trickled down his neck as he slogged back to the house, his limp daughter in his arms.

"This isn't real!" Dora cried from the porch. She had believed Billy was immune to this sort of tragedy. He had already paid his dues; the hay truck had taken care of that. "This isn't real!"

Hours later, Billy pushed through the darkness to his tractor. He climbed up and started the engine, his chest heaving. Felt like his lungs might crack through his ribs. Sat there awhile, looking up at the swarm of stars, breathing in the stink of mud.

Dora moved with numb determination that night. She searched for everything that was Charlotte's—toys, clothes, little forks and spoons, picture books—and packed it all away in the tornado cellar. When Billy finally returned, he found Dora at the kitchen table, pounding away at the typewriter.

No animosity. No bickering. Just a season of empty silence. Billy didn't sell the farm; he let it rot, bought a shack near Lake Arrowhead. Dora retreated to Connect-icut for a few months, then returned to Texas and found an apartment in Wichita Falls not unlike the one she had rented when she first started at the *Journal*.

Billy moved through his days slowly, tending to a few culture beds, selling bait in Chinese takeout boxes. He combed the newspapers: the *Journal*, plus two from Dallas, and on Thursdays the Sunday *New York Times* arrived in the mail. WRECK KILLS HONOR STUDENT, TWO OTHERS—maybe. TRENTON MOTHER RUNS OVER INFANT SON IN DRIVEWAY—yes. NOTED POET HANGS HIMSELF—not even close. AFTER SIX-YEAR SEARCH, ADOPTED TEEN LEARNS BIOLOGICAL MOTHER DIED AT HIS BIRTH—Billy thought yes at first, but the kid's adoptive parents seemed nice, and he was living a good life with two siblings, private schools, a German shepherd. Billy wondered why he'd read the entire article: waste of time. LOS ANGELES WOMAN, SIX MONTHS PREGNANT, STABBED TO DEATH IN PARKING LOT— yes. Easily, yes. The yesses he tacked to the wall around his bathroom mirror. They yellowed and curled, a dirty mane around his face each morning as he shaved and brushed his teeth.

He nailed Charlotte's painting of the worm onto the wall in the kitchen. Next to it hung the portrait of himself—Dora had never asked for it, never even mentioned it. When she returned to the farmhouse from up north she had only gathered her books, two typewriters, and clothes.

Dora resumed work at the *Journal,* continued to write profiles. Despite blanketing the country with her manuscripts and clippings, she had no more bites from national magazines. A different rejection note each time: *Too quirky. Who cares? Not quirky enough. Boring.* But these notes didn't discourage her, didn't upset her. They piled up on the counter in her kitchenette. She decided that when she finally sold another profile to a major magazine, she'd use the rejections to make a papier-mâché piñata that she'd fill with walnuts and kumquats—Louise's favorites. She'd blast Janis Joplin on her hi-fi, and she and Louise would bust open the piñata with her umbrella, then light candles and lie in bed all day, feeding each other.

Louise and Dora had met in a European history course in their second year of college. They fell together during exam week at the end of every semester, helped each other relax, discussed popes and treaties and the oppressed. Proofread, quizzed, baked banana bread, burned incense, massaged each other.

The letter from Louise had been at the bottom of the stack of mail that greeted Dora when she returned to work: *I heard from Bunny Perkins that you lived up there in Wichita Falls and wrote for the paper. If you can believe it, I'm down in Dallas, married to a rich (oil) bastard of a man, a hateful fat thing who smokes cigars and eats pork every night. Are you as bored as I am?*

Dora hadn't thought of Louise in years, but the note sent a warm, calming wave through her body. She called immediately.

When Dora came to visit, Billy would meet her on his buckling and heel-gnawed front porch. During the hot months, he'd prepare a pitcher of iced tea and they'd drink it down, watch the sun sparkle on the lake, shoo a horsefly or two. Dora sensed Billy didn't want her inside his little house, knew not to ask, not to push, but she wondered what was in there. Billy would talk of worms, how he was think-ing of moving back to the farm, maybe trying to get

the business going again. He had new ideas for spe-
cialized hybrids, worms raised in higher-saline soil
that would wiggle more when hooked and thrown
into fresh water. When he spoke of these plans, his
eyes would widen and shift wildly; he'd spit a little
through the chip in his tooth. "I think I finally got
it all figured out," he said one day, "I just got to
drive down to the farm."

"I bet you could do it, Billy," Dora lied.

He knew she was humoring him, knew he sounded
like a nut; his ideas were ridiculous. Why couldn't he
stop babbling? Why couldn't he simply have a pleasant conversation with his beautiful wife? No worm
talk. Maybe, if he asked politely, they could just sit
out there, and he could look at her like he used to, and
neither would have to say anything. He could stand in
awe of her. She could relax. The few times he had
touched her since Charlotte died, when he merely
tried to run his thumb along her jaw or push her hair
out of her eyes, Dora pulled away. She never said anything, but her tightened posture told him he repulsed
her.

As usual, she brought her latest clippings, folded
neatly in a manila envelope. But he would never read
them. He'd wad them up, envelope and all, and toss
them in the culture bed. Worm food. He preferred the
tragedies.

Dora wished Billy would move on, offered to drive him to the farm in Olney herself, but he said no, looked down at the splintering planks between his boots.

She knew she was lucky that Louise appeared when she did, and hoped that someone might fall from the sky for Billy. Said so.

"What do you mean?" he asked.

"I mean everyone should have someone to love," she said.

"I have you."

"No," she said. "You don't really."

He sighed through the hole in his bite. "I know that," he said. "I've known that for a while. You shouldn't have to come over here every week. You're busy."

"I like coming over here," she said. Her visits both mitigated and intensified her guilt—a sickening paradox. "What can I do for you?" she asked. She grabbed his hand, which was no longer rough and callused but smooth, a little clammy. "What can I do?"

"Shove me out of the way," he said, thoughts squirming madly through his mind. "Please, just shove me out of the way."

Gators

I've been watching Durina grow since she was five years old. I'm not a pervert or anything, although I admit I watched her more closely and a little too frequently when she entered those new-woman years from eleven to fourteen. Admired her even, like I admire the women on the nighttime soap operas. Her body so new—just discovering what to do with it, learning about its power.

But I stopped that business. Felt wrong.

Went against everything I learned. Earned my Class D Education Certificate at the junior college when I was twenty-seven. Three nights a week for two years, including the summers. Sent in all the necessary paperwork, was fingerprinted at the courthouse, and registered with the school system. I can substitute up to ninety days per school year, coach, direct, tutor, help out on field trips, drive a school bus if I get my chauffeur's license renewed—everything except have my own classroom and teach. I'd need two more years of college for that.

I tutored Durina in reading from grades one through four, and judged the elementary-school science fair, which she won for WHY DOES COKE MAKE NAILS RUST SO FAST? I was the soccer coach for her junior-high years, and Durina was the only girl on the team. She was the best at all the positions—not that I knew the positions. The coaches from Belle Rose and Pigeon, our opponents, they didn't know the positions, either. We all knew soccer players can't use their hands. We all knew about out-of-bounds. And we all decided that each team should have between four and seven players on the field during the game, which we decided lasted forty-five minutes—three fifteen-minute periods with one extra period if the score is tied. We're not dumb, just lazy—which I admit. And those were the rules we agreed on.

The other coaches, Chuck and Pet, drank beers with me at the It'll Do Tavern on Saturday evenings after the games. Pet once said something about Durina, something about her coming from the Isle of

Lesbos, so I swatted his face with my coaching stats book. "Saying that about a sixth-grade girl! Saying that about Durina!" My book left a burning red rectangle on his cheek. Then I shoved him off his stool and stepped on his neck, making him feel like he couldn't breathe.

I said, "Look, Pet, you don't know her and you never will. You're not even qualified to be on the same field as Durina. Not as a coach. Not as a player, and not as a coach of the opposing team, and not as a waterboy or a cheerleader—if we had them."

All this time Pet was gurgling like a sick baby, and I was pressing harder and twisting my heel.

Eventually I took my boot up, apologized to the people in the tavern for the ruckus. Felt bad about Pet, lying on the sticky sawdusty floor, red and sweaty, his T-shirt hiked up so you could see his doughy white stomach, his deep navel. So I bought him an It'll Do windbreaker, which he wears just about every chance he gets. Twelve dollars. Pet never said anything like that about Durina again. Probably won't ever.

I was Durina's substitute ceramics teacher when she was in ninth grade, and I directed her in *West Side Story* that following summer. She was a girl Jet. I've seen her grow into the brightest flower this parish has ever produced.

Durina likes shoes. Makes her own. Slippers, clogs, mules, pumps, slingbacks, sandals, flats, boots. All kinds. Has since she could hold a hammer and sneak into the drying shed and pull the skins from the bags. Her mother, Honey, works the gator business. Guts the gators right there behind their house. Slits them down their backs, salts the skins, rolls them, hangs them in canvas bags for the buyers to inspect them. Louisiana skins. No nubbed marks, no scabby button bumps like the sorry-ass Florida skins. Just smooth, uninterrupted alligator skin.

Sad that no one knows who Durina's daddy is. Some say it's an Indian, an Indian from Arizona with a made-up Indian name like Climbing Bear or Dancing Frog or Turkey Feather or Geronimo. They say Honey—who we know for sure is Durina's mother because we saw her pregnant—met him when she and her daddy drove six days to the Grand Canyon. The Indian was sitting there in the red dust on a woven blanket, selling turquoise jewelry, and soon Honey, with her big eyes and bigger hips, struck his fancy.

He porked her in a mud hut, they say. Or in a teepee.

The pregnancy just about killed Honey's daddy—Durina's granddaddy—because he knew it was that Indian and he blamed himself for taking Honey out of Louisiana even if it was to see something as important as the Grand Canyon.

But Band-Aids down at the post office swears Durina's daddy was the Cuban who sold Honey's daddy the old veiny-legged mule they still keep in the back. The mule became their property just a few weeks after they returned from the Grand Canyon. It bit Honey's daddy on the shoulder with its giant mule teeth, and the infection he got was the first stage of his demise. Had a yellow arm for the months preceding his death. I saw the yellow arm myself when I was a teenager. Yellow as left-out butter. The Cuban hung around town just long enough to lay into Honey once or twice. Band-Aids claims to have seen them going at it down by the creek. She says the Cuban had a big tattoo of the Virgin Mary on his back, and Honey was digging her nails into the Holy Mother's face, making the Holy Mother cry blood like a miracle in Italy. The Cuban left town just as smoothly as he had come in, never to be seen again. We remember him each time we see the mule.

Now, the Cuban story is from Band-Aids, as I said. Take it or leave it, because Band-Aids is unbalanced. Demented, even. She covers her arms with Band-Aids whether she's got cuts or not. Has done it since I can remember. Always has at least five stuck on each arm. Isn't ashamed of her problem, either. Her uniform there at the P.O. is short-sleeved. I used to ask her, "What happened to your arms?" and she'd say her cat got her, or she'd say she was trimming back her rose bushes. Once, she said, "You'll never believe this, Vaughn, but a package came in from Texas yesterday, and it was swarming with fire ants that bit me up!" She had stuck Band-Aids on her neck and face, too, that day.

I've seen the steering wheel of Band-Aids's truck: completely covered with Band-Aids.

Durina's skin is the color of caramel, and her eyes are as dark as mud, so she could be either half-Indian or half-Cuban. Then there's the Creole possibility. Whoever it was that knocked up Honey must have had a beautiful mother of his own because Honey is certainly no prize.

Durina used to wear her dark hair long, down past her shoulders. But her mother drove her into New Orleans a few years back, and Durina returned sporting a short pixie cut with a navy blue tint. Since then, she's gone through many color phases, but her hair remains short. Lately, it's been bleached out and messed. She could have a foot-deep purple Afro or a shaved head and she'd still be beautiful.

The shoe designers fly down from New York or fly over from Paris. They used to send buyers down, but now they come themselves and pretend like they know a thing or two about gator skin when they're looking through the bags in Honey's drying shed. One designer, James, a big nellie, white, but with natty hair like a poor black child's, he started to come down about ten years ago, and the shoes and purses he made were such hits in the fashion world that twenty or so designers, most of them nellies, too—even the married nellies with their skinny big-lipped pretend wives— came on down in packs that next year.

Honey had hired seven men. Skinned more gators in that one season than she had in the ten before—combined. The odor filled the town like a substance. On some afternoons everything we ate tasted of rotten gator. Catfish: gator. Popcorn: gator. Pizza: gator. Coca-Cola: gator.

Honey'll sell the meat, too, sometimes, but most of the time it's not worth the trouble. People eat gator when they have to, and lately, no one around here has been that desperate. A few tourists or college kids on road trips sometimes buy it, but locals rarely do. Even stewed and spiced up, it tastes like an old baseball mitt.

Durina's been showing the designers her shoes from the start, since she was a little thing. But the designers dismiss her, saying things like, "Those are cute, dear." I keep thinking that if Durina were a boy, those nellies would have invited her (him) right up to New York by now. They'd have her (him) design shoes, and they would expect a few favors in return for the opportunity they'd given her (him)—favors their skinny big-lipped supermodel wives couldn't do for them.

But Durina's shoes get better and better. Every year. That's where she is now. Putting the finishing touches on several different pairs to show the designers who'll be here soon.

Honey only does the cutting, salting, and rolling of the skins. Leaves the rest of the skin processing for whoever buys it. But all those designers know Honey kills the best gators, so they'll shell out and hire more people to finish the skin processing.

When Durina makes a pair of shoes, she does all of the processing herself. Every step. Digs her own lime pits, places the skins in them until the back scales and spines practically flake off. She pickles the skins. She tans them. She dyes them. She glazes them, and finally, she polishes them. I don't even want to think about the chemicals she's exposed to. I don't want to think about the flipper-armed earless babies she might have in the future. There are plenty of guys around here who could process the skins for Durina, plenty of guys who've already been poisoned, whose eyes are loose, whose skin is gritty and oily even after a bath, whose genes are scrambled, but Durina won't let anyone do it but herself. She says that she's the only one left in this parish who knows the final, secret stage of processing: the Bombé Treatment. I'm not familiar with all the details, but I know the Bombé Treatment involves shining up the skin with heat—Durina uses a blow dryer—and buffing it with the skin of another animal. I don't know which animal. Durina won't tell me. It could be anything: deer, dog, rabbit, squirrel, bird, camel . . . When you rub the gator skins she's worked on, you'd swear you were rubbing pudding or some other solid thing that's so smooth it's almost a liquid. Durina could make alligator skin underpants and you'd be comfortable in them even if they were a size too small.

My family didn't do gators. They didn't fish, either, or work in the cancer factories on the river. My daddy built up a small carnival from nothing but a pair of trained monkeys he had traded with a man for one steel-belted radial tire—when those tires were first invented. The pictures from then are curled and faded, but not so much that you can't make out the monkeys. They wore hats and wigs, and people on their way from New Orleans to Donaldsonville would stop and hand them nickels. The monkeys would turn back flips or kiss each other after a mock wedding ceremony, and the people would give them more nickels.

In a drawer around here I have one of the monkeys'

hands, shriveled and attached to a small keychain. Daddy never let me call it a hand.

"It's a paw," he'd say. "Not a hand."

"Why?"

"Hands are human, Vaughn. Monkeys are animals."

"They have four fingers and a thumb."

"Five paw parts. Five claws."

Now that my daddy's dead, I call the hand a hand. It's sad, looks like a hairy prune, and I don't much like it, anyway. I don't believe it has voodoo power or it's cursed, but I leave it there in the drawer and rarely touch it, just in case.

The first carnival ride Daddy bought was the Ferris Wheel. Seats twenty to thirty. Made enough money off that to buy a Merry-Go-Round, then a Tilt-a-Whirl, then the Looping Hammerhead Rockets. I turned on the rides one summer after Daddy passed, made several hundred dollars off tickets in July alone. About fifty visitors a night. Mostly drunk kids from the four-year Baptist college up the road.

But I don't know as much about engines and mechanics as Daddy did, and I was afraid someone might fly out of their seat and bust open their head, especially one of those sorority girls. Put a few beers in a sorority girl, and she's standing up on the Tilt-a-Whirl, or throwing up on the rockets. I've kept the rides off since that summer. They rust. They clang in the breeze. The sun and rain have leached their paint of its brightness. The Tilt-a-Whirl seats used to be red. Now they're more the color of Silly Putty. Weeds and kudzu grow over the Merry-Go-Round. You can barely see the horses. It looks like a giant shrub, and I swear about thirty nutria live in there, including an albino one. The rides are eyesores, I know, and one of these days, I'll drag out Daddy's tools and fix them up, get them rolling for one last summer, put up signs on the highway, because I know Durina will never have enough money in New York.

Durina shoves open the screen door and bounds into my kitchen where I sit at the table flipping through the fat heavy *Vogue* I just got in my mailbox. The perfume from the magazine, all forty-seven scents, is almost too much on an empty stomach, but I put up with it for Durina's sake. I'm the only other person in town who subscribes to *Vogue*. April twenty-fifth today, and it's the summer preview issue. Thicker than last year's, but not even close to the fall preview issue. Durina's clutching her own under her arm. She lays it flat on the blue Formica and opens to a Gucci ad, smoothing her thumb over a dark photo of a pouting girl in underwear. A pouting boy in black pants who looks more like a girl than the pouting girl except he's got no breasts, this boy has the girl's hair in his pouting mouth. The pouting girl's shoes are chunky boots. The pouting boy wears square-toed loafers with more of a heel than should be on a man's shoe.

"I don't know what Tom Ford's thinking," Durina says. "These are the tiredest things I've seen since the neo-post-retro eighties bullshit last year."

"I thought that, too," I say. "And did you see the photo spread on the last few pages? The volcano one?"

"No one," Durina says, "no one no one no one no one will ever wear those knee-high strap-ups." She blows a rogue strand of hair out of her eyes. "I'm awash in disappointment."

"Whatever happened to skin innovation?"

"Exactly," she says. "I know what these chicks with this look need on their feet, and it's not what they're wearing now."

"What do they need?" I ask, and she goes on to tell me, her eyes bugging a little, her breathing picking up. She pulls her pencil kit and pad from her bag and quickly sketches a few shoes: simple stacked-heel ankle-high boots, in a cherry-black color. Sleek. Mod. I picture her giving a presentation in front of a group of important designers and critics: men with crew cuts in turtleneck sweaters. Women with drastic bobs, severe lipstick. They all stand and clap when Durina's finished. There's a low mumbling, in French, a few laughs, and finally one guy walks over to Durina and kisses her on each of her cheeks.

"Welcome," he says with a heavy, maybe bogus, accent.

"No one is dyeing gator like they should," Durina tells me, slapping her pencil down on the table. "It's so easy, and no one's doing it."

"Show me your new shoes," I say.

"Not yet," she says.

"When?"

"Soon," she says, twirling her pencil. Coy. "It seems like you're too into all this," she adds.

"I just want to see the shoes." I do. "Take out your homework."

The administrators at the high school called Honey into the office one afternoon, told her that Durina's shoes were distracting to other students. Honey sat there, probably stinking of gator, shirt blooming with gator blood, and told Mr. Hanover, the principal, she told him his light blue button-down-collared shirt was distracting her. She couldn't concentrate on what he was saying because the shirt was driving her crazy. Then she stood and walked out. I heard this from Honey herself, over supper that night. I had caught a couple of catfish, one about the size of Shaquille O'Neal's shoe, the other, smaller, for Durina, and I brought them over before Honey put something else on the stove.

"That's what I told him," Honey said. "Then I walked

out."

"I tried that," Durina said, "but it didn't work. I told Mrs. Fulmer that her pull-on double-knit pants were distracting me because I knew how much her thighs must hurt chafing around in them, but she said my shoes were monstrosities and sent me to the office."

So I told Durina: "You go right ahead and wear those clogs to school, and if anyone says anything, I'll speak to them. But don't go lipping off to anyone, not even Mrs. Fulmer. Now give me some more of that dirty rice, please."

The suppers over there had to stop about a year ago. Honey got to be too much. The last time—the time I told myself no more, no way—that time, Honey sauntered up to me in the kitchen as I was washing the dishes, and she pressed herself against my rump, and smiled in that way that you knew she was feeling something down there where her legs meet, she was feeling something at your expense. Then she reached around and grabbed my private right through my pants and kneaded it. My hands were up, suds rolling off my elbows and plooping on the floor, and she was going at it, rubbing herself on my leg and still squeezing and massaging me through my pants. I wanted to say something, but my voice didn't work, and soon— even though I was focusing hard on the big flakes of scalp skin on the sunburnt part in her hair, and I was smelling the onions and fish on her breath and the gator on her clothes, and I was hearing her wet thick breathing—she moved it just the right way, activated that one charged-up part, and I lost it in my pants and made a few noises like a baby animal might make if you stepped on it.

Driving home with a mess in my pants, I prayed Officer Poimboeuf wouldn't pull me over as he often did for no reason. I couldn't stand the sogginess, and I almost stopped the car and ripped off my pants and put them in the trunk. Then I thought if Poimboeuf did pull me over, he'd sure notice if I had no pants, but he might not notice the wet circle growing bigger and bigger—although he loved to shine his long black flashlight into the car. I guess I could have spread a map over my lap, or pulled into the Dairy Whip and got a cone from the drive-thru and on-purpose dropped it onto my pants so the wet spot would look like melted ice cream.

Someone finally gut-shot that bastard Poimboeuf a few months back. Left him to rot under a bridge after he pulled them over. Poimboeuf didn't die, but now he's got to wear adult diapers. And don't think people around here have any pity on him, because they don't, and they'll yell things at him from their cars when they see him. He grew a beard, but people still recognize him. Can't miss him. His head's shaped like an eggplant, and with the adult diapers, he makes a crinkle noise when he walks.

I made it home that night without being pulled over by Poimboeuf, without having to stop at the Dairy Whip and drop a cone on my lap. But I did quit having suppers over there with Honey and Durina. When Durina asks me about it, I tell her that her mother has too many responsibilities and she doesn't need to be fixing supper for another mouth, my mouth. Honey needs to be concentrating on Durina, getting Durina settled in New York next year. Honey ought not to be grabbing men like she does. She never could find just one man, the right man. I could list about fifty different men around here who've known her in the biblical sense. I could list them right off the top of my head if I had to. If I went into the It'll Do, filled my mouth with beer, spun around, and spit it out, ten or twenty men who've been in Honey's bed would be wiping foam from their eyes. I suspect Durina knows about Honey's man-shopping. Durina deserves a better mother.

Nowadays, I'm focusing on letting Durina have as much time as she needs to finish her shoes before the nellie parade marches down. So we'll sit at my kitchen table and speed through her homework each afternoon. It's her final semester in high school and she only has three academic classes: French, Trigonometry, and British Literature. I own the teacher's edition of her English book, and her teacher, Mrs. Fulmer, is as lazy as she is ugly and doesn't stray from the exercises in the book. Durina knows all about Lord Byron, and Shakespeare, and Chaucer—knows as much as her teacher. The answers are right there in blue lettering. Durina copies them verbatim, and Mrs. Fulmer doesn't notice, or doesn't care. The French, I can't help her with, but her French teacher, Monsieur Babcock, he's lazy, too. He doesn't like to grade papers, so he's always having his students perform impromptu skits and awarding them arbitrary grades. Durina gets all A's from him on account of her bringing in stacks of glossy French magazines and decorating Monsieur Babcock's classroom with images of anorexic French girls draped in haute couture. We actually do the trigonometry. I convinced Durina to take it, so I feel obligated to help. She's smart, anyway. I hardly have to help.

Lately, Durina's hands have been stained a new color each day from the dyes and tanning chemicals. She needs to stop that about a week before the designers get here so she doesn't have green or red or brown or purple hands and look like a freak. Because those designers only care about one thing: appearance—and they're not going to buy shoe designs from a girl with dirty hands. "Presentable," I tell her.

"There's this movement," Durina tells me after she closes her trigonometry book, "where people are going to Indian women—like women from India, not Native Americans—to have their hands and feet painted with henna."

"I read the same magazines you do," I tell her. "I know about those hand painters. I saw a picture of Sting having his feet painted."

"I could dye each of my fingers a different shade with food coloring. Food coloring is safe."

"You could," I say. "But don't."

"Why?"

"Just don't," I say. "Take my word for it. Those designers copy stuff from kids your age, they steal the trends from you guys, but they don't want to buy ideas from you. They wouldn't trust a girl with rainbow fingers to design shoes. They wouldn't take her seriously. But they'll make the half-dead twelve-year-old junkie model in their next shoot dye her fingers different colors."

"I'll do what I want," she says. "My designs this year are amazing. They'll speak for themselves."

"We need to think about when you're moving up there," I say. "We need to figure out where you're gonna live. Lots of people just starting out live in Brooklyn."

"Chelsea," she says.

"And how much money do you have saved?"

"I'll have enough in July," she says.

"You'll need a few thousand at least."

"Haven't we talked about this before?" she says. "Aren't I sick of this topic?"

We have talked about this before. A million times. What she doesn't know is that I have almost five thousand in the bank for her. I've been saving since she was in elementary school. I don't want her to know this, because I don't want her to stop working as hard as she can. I don't want her to lose her passion for shoes. Part of this passion comes from a survival instinct that would die if she knew I had the money for her. She'd spend it all on shoes the first week she got to New York. There'd be pyramids of shoe boxes stacked to the ceiling in her apartment. Actually, the shoes Durina admires the most, the ones designed by Salvatore Ferragamo, Bruno Magli (the traditionalists), or Stephane Kelian (the only one close, Durina says, to being innovative with skins) must go for four or five hundred a pair, I think, so there would only be ten or fifteen boxes in her apartment, hardly enough for a pyramid. I'll go up there with her, I'll drive her myself, and I'll make sure she's all set. Someone has to do it, and I know Honey won't.

There's an unwritten fact of life I've noticed: All

successful people leave home when they're eighteen. Seventeen's too early. Nineteen's too late. Around here, most everyone fits into the too-late category. Now, I'm not saying they're bad people, or that they're particularly unhappy or criminal here in this parish, because they're not. I'm just saying that they'll never be in *Time* magazine, not even mentioned, unless they gun down a famous person. They'll never meet anyone smarter than them, or better-looking, or even anyone who wasn't born in this parish. And they'll never really want to do much else than live out their lives here, getting excited about the new flavors of potato chips that show up at the 7-Eleven, and listening to the same old Lynyrd Skynyrd tapes as they're parked by the pond. I know this because I didn't leave until I was twenty-three. I went to Florida to work for only a summer, poisoning caterpillars. And now here I am, approaching forty a little too quickly, living in my dead daddy's house where I always have. I could've stayed in Florida, found another job after the poisoning work ran out, but I didn't. The whole time I was gone, I was thinking about coming home. Thought so hard about how much I missed home, felt like I'd been punched in the stomach. I missed the dumbest things: the squish of mud under the slabs that lead up to my front porch from the sidewalk, the green smell of Bird Pond, my pillow, the crooked sign at the liquor store—all things I would have made fun of someone else for missing.

Just as Durina yawns and begins to pack up her things tonight, Pet knocks on the door and walks into the kitchen. He's wearing the It'll Do windbreaker I bought him, clutching a six-pack of Dixie to his chest. He plops the beer on the counter, removes his ball cap, and says hello to Durina, who's gathering the last of her colored pencils.

"You don't have to remove your cap on my account," Durina says. "Vaughn here never does."

"I do, too," I say. "Sometimes."

"I always remove my cap in the presence of a pretty lady," Pet says. "I was brought up right." He grins. A triangle is chipped from his top teeth. His eyes trace around Durina's body, linger on her breasts. I could kill him sometimes, punch another hole in his smile.

"I like your boots," Durina tells Pet as she squeezes by him on out the door. And from the yard she yells, "You two perverts have fun with that porno tape." She laughs and skips off.

"How in the name of screaming Jesus did she know?" Pet asks, pulling the tape out from under his windbreaker. *Federal Sexpress:* The delivery guy bones each of the women in a high-powered law firm until they all realize he's a dirty seven-timing dog and they kidnap him. Then they torture him with feathers. It ends in a messy, severely degrading orgy. Pet's brought this tape over at least three times before.

"Let's watch normal TV," I say, but we end up drinking the beer at the kitchen table and not watching anything. Sweat beads gather on the cans and on our foreheads, get heavy, then drip onto the Formica. Tonight Pet's talking about his summer plans, where he's fixing to go when he finishes his Pee Wee Baseball coaching. This time it's Mexico. He's heard about a small fishing village where hotel rooms are ten bucks a night and Corona beer is a quarter a bottle. Tourists rent sea kayaks and paddle out to islands where women sunbathe without tops. Last summer he said he was going up to Washington, D.C., to see all the monuments and visit all the museums: "It's about time I take advantage of all the things my federal tax dollars have been maintaining for all these years." He never went to D.C., and he'll not go to Mexico, but I don't say anything tonight. If I were drunker, and in a worse mood, I might say something. I might tell him to shut the hell up, and to start warming up his VCR's remote control because all he's going to do this summer is sit at home and watch the same three porno tapes and sweat all over his plaid couch.

But I let him go on about Mexico, how in July everything there's even cheaper because the average daily temperature is one hundred and twelve degrees, how he can take the heat better than anyone because he's read up on bodily water control or some bullshit like that.

All this time I'm thinking that in July I should be helping Durina move into her place in Brooklyn, or, if she has her way and she's lucky, Chelsea. I wonder what her place will look like: carpeting or hardwood floors? Shower or bathtub? Western, eastern, southern, or northern exposure? And I wonder about her neighbors: An old Jewish couple? A fast-talking club kid like I've seen on the talk shows? A somber graduate student with poor hygiene? An aged hooker?

I can make myself crazy wondering, creating scenarios. I'm in the middle of a dinner party thrown by the old Jewish couple where the graduate student— his name is Justin, he's wearing a COLUMBIA T-shirt with a hole at the neck—is berating Durina for working in an industry set on oppressing and exploiting women. He says something about Chinese women binding their feet. I see there are candles on the table, and heaps of mashed potatoes, and the old Jewish man is wearing a blue tie that clashes with his brown suit. Plastic fruit magnets hold notes and coupons to their refrigerator door. Before Durina responds to the graduate student's onslaught, Pet asks, "Huh?" and shakes my shoulder.

"What?" I say.

"You want to go with me? I'm getting the plane tickets next week."

"I'm busy this summer," I say.

"You turning on the rides again?"

"Might just. One last time."

"The Band-Aid lady said you were buying a new ride this summer," Pet says.

"Did she say that?"

"She says you got more than five thousand in your bank account."

"She's lying," I lie.

If I mail something to Boston or Los Angeles, or if I receive a package from Maine or Oregon, the ladies at the bank know about it. In return, Band-Aids at the post office is privy to the balances of my checking and savings accounts. The girl who works at Dr. Marhan's office—her name's Tina but everyone calls her Tiny because she's a giant thing with spidery hands and feet like a basketball player's—she knows the bank ladies, so they all knew when I had the warts removed from my armpits and asked me if it hurt one day when I went in there to make a deposit. I told them that Tiny had misinformed them. I hadn't had warts removed from my armpits. I had them removed from somewhere more private.

"You really gonna turn the rides on?" Pet asks.

"Might." I don't want to. I'd rather take them apart like I said. But there is money to be had, money Durina might need in New York. I could pay Durina to run the Ferris Wheel, and Pet could run the Tilt-a-Whirl. Better for him than sitting in the house and masturbating the summer away. I could pay both of them to give the rides fresh coats of paint before the summer begins. I could pay Pet twenty bucks to test ride the Hammerhead Rockets.

I was ten years old when the big truck brought the Hammerhead Rockets. It was early in the morning, and the squeal and hiss of the eighteen-wheeler's brakes woke me. I looked outside into the pink light just before sunrise and saw the truck: A AND L AMUSEMENTS. Ran out there into the cool air in my underpants and slippers, the cold dewy grass wetting my ankles.

Daddy said to me, "This here is the first ride in this parish to turn its riders completely upside down." Then he kneeled down, grabbed onto my bare shoulders with his rough callused hands, looked right into my eyes, and said, "Do you understand the significance of this?"

"Yes," I lied.

"Do you really?" He didn't blink. In that morning light, his eyes were gray, the color of wet cement. Usually they were more the color of ice.

"I think I do."

"After you ride the rockets, you'll know," he said. "You'll know how important this is."

A few hours later, I was looping through the sky, caged in one of the rockets. And I remember thinking way back then that the rockets weren't that scary, that the Ferris Wheel, the way it swayed in the slightest wind, the way it creaked, was much scarier. The rockets were boring, even on that premier ride. Too smooth. Of course, I didn't tell my daddy that. When I got off that first time, I said, "Being upside down is scarier than I thought."

"You're a brave boy taking that virgin flight," Daddy said.

"I want to ride again," I said. "Can you make them go faster?"

"You're a real brave boy, Vaughn," he said. That's what he had said about a year earlier, right before he told me that my mother had fallen out of the rowboat and drowned in Bird Pond. He had used the same exact words: You're a real brave boy, Vaughn.

Band-Aids claimed my mother had tied burlap bags full of rocks to her ankles and drowned herself when she learned my daddy was having an affair with a black woman who lived in the woods near Pigeon. I was just nine years old when she told me. It was just a few days after they buried my mother. I had been happily riding my bike downtown, enjoying the week off the principal had granted me to recover from my mother's death, and Band-Aids actually ran out of the post office, her official-looking black oxford shoes slapping the sidewalk. She yelled for me to stop, just so she could tell me. "That Negro woman got a ring in her nose, and she don't wear shoes," Band-Aids said to me, her chicken eyes looking this way and that. "And she's been sinning with your daddy in a carnal way." An old Band-Aid had found its way into her stacked-up hair. It hung off the side of her head there like a Christmas ornament someone had forgotten to take off a dry brown Christmas tree. "Fornicate like swine, the two of them do!" I rode home real quick and looked up *fornicate* and *carnal* in the dictionary. I had a good idea what *fornicate* meant, but I looked it up anyway because, back then, seeing even the most vaguely sexual words in print was a thrill.

I never mustered up enough courage to ask Daddy if it was true about the shoeless black lady. I thought about asking him when he was sick, when I knew he was about to die, but I figured it didn't really matter. I suspect it was true. I once walked behind the Tilt-a-Whirl to find my babysitter, Cheryl Toussaint, on her knees in front of Daddy. His pants down around his ankles, white ass cheeks bunching up, angry-sounding grunts. Even before my mother died, women would call the house at all hours. They'd be surprised if I answered, and they'd say things like "I suppose you have a mommy, too" or "I should have known." My mother knew about my daddy's philandering. If I knew, she knew. She had other things to worry about, secret worries, important worries. I didn't see that she cared about my father. So I doubt that's why she drowned herself—if she did drown herself.

Durina graduated from high school last night. Stomped like Frankenstein's monster across the stage to receive her diploma wearing some killer platforms I had never seen before.

"I want to know about the platforms," I tell her. "Are you showing them to the designers next week?" Durina and I are sitting on her mother's porch, drinking down iced tea and watching the heat rise up from the lush grass in visible waves that distort everything behind them. I figure as long as Honey's out slicing up gators, I'm safe, but I keep thinking she'll be home any second, which scares me. Usually when Honey comes home, she comes through the back, and the mule whinnies and snorts when he sees her, so I'm warned, and I can leave before she lays her mitts on me.

"James will be down tomorrow, and three more guys are coming down on Thursday—this week, not next week," she says.

"You ready?"

"I've been ready my whole life."

"Why can't I see them?"

"Patience, Vaughn."

"How many do you have?"

"Three, other than the platforms, which I might not show to them." She plucks an ice cube from her glass and runs it across her throat, then her forehead. She tosses the ice at a sparrow that has lighted on the sorry little caterpillar-ravaged peach tree that Honey tries to keep alive with mule shit.

"I just want things to work out for you," I say. "I don't trust any of the designers."

"Sometimes, Vaughn—and I don't mean to be cruel or ungrateful, really—but sometimes I think you should try helping yourself as much as you help me. Maybe you should try to focus less on me. I'm almost eighteen now, you know."

"I know that," I say, but before I can finish responding, the screen door opens and Honey's standing behind me. Her moist hands on my shoulders, her thumbs massaging my sweaty neck. I didn't hear the mule. I didn't even hear Honey walking toward the door—and it's all hardwood floors, and she's wearing cowboy boots. No warning. "I gotta go," I say, standing, placing my glass of tea on the little wicker table.

"But I just finished hanging the skins," Honey

whines. "We got some beautiful ones today, and I wanted to celebrate by making you two dinner. You haven't stayed for dinner in a long time, Vaughn." She's got a blob of dark gator blood congealing in her hair, and her shirt is unbuttoned a little too far. No bra on Honey. Plenty of freckles.

"I've been busy," I tell her. "And I gotta help my friend Pet with his truck tonight when it cools off a little." I wipe the sweat from my brow for show.

"You can't do that tomorrow? Invite Pet over for dinner tonight. I haven't seen that old boy in a while."

"Yes," Durina says. "Invite Pet over. Tell him to wear those sweet-ass logger boots. I need to check out the stitching."

"I'm sorry," I say, backing off the porch, "but Pet's truck's real bad off and he's teaching tennis lessons out at the day camp so he needs it fixed right away."

"Maybe I'll catch you boys some night at the It'll Do when we finish up this gator season," Honey says. Then she flicks her tongue at me. Durina doesn't see.

"Okay, then," I say. "Durina, I sure do appreciate the tea. See you tomorrow?"

"Right," she says.

"Bye, dear," Honey says.

Of course I'm not helping Pet with his truck tonight. He's probably at home, cuddling up to his VCR, ten or fifteen empty beer cans on the floor in front of him, some crunched, some not.

I'm greasing the Hammerhead Rockets, the easiest of the rides to maintain. Only twelve security bolts to check and none seems that badly rusted. I try not to think about how many years it's been since I turned them on. The belts are dried and will snap soon, so I'll run over to the auto parts store tomorrow and pick up some new ones. Durina's never ridden them. She said so once a few years back. Also said, "Of all those old rusted rides, that looping one seems like the best."

"Daddy said it was, and he knew the rides better than anyone."

"Some day when I'm a famous shoe designer, I'll insist on a photo shoot here."

"This would be a good place for a photo shoot."

"I'll ride all of them," she said, lazily pointing. "Have you ever noticed that famous people never die on carnival rides?"

"They never ride carnival rides," I told her, but now I think harder about what she said. If fame is what Durina wants, and if she thinks fame will make her invincible, she's wrong. Sonny Bono and a Kennedy died in skiing accidents, and there was that dancer whose scarf got caught in the wheel spokes of her sports car and strangled her. But Durina's right about one thing: there has never been a celebrity amusement park or carnival death.

The air has cooled, the humidity has settled, and the crickets' chirping is so thick it feels as if they're inside me, like a few might hop from my ears and mouth. With those new belts and a few lightbulbs, the rockets could be ready tomorrow night. I could have Pet test-ride them in the afternoon, and I'll have Durina over tomorrow evening after we meet with James about her shoes. I'll surprise her by turning on the ride. I'll blindfold her, lead her out into the yard, turn on all the rockets' lights, and say, "Voilà!" as I untie the bandanna.

I'll stop myself here before the scenario becomes more elaborate.

A few years back, I got to wondering about my mother too often. It got so I couldn't go down to Bird Pond. I'd picture her, thrashing around under the murky water, the sunbeams pushing through, glowing green. The bags of rocks are tied to her ankles. She thinks of me, a soon-to-be motherless child, changes her mind, struggles to undo the knots. She gets one bag off, but the other's knots are too tight. Her lungs burn with water. Her mouth moves like she's breathing. Everything swirls and twinkles, goes purple, then black.

Truth is, I don't believe my mother had the energy to think much about me. Her eyes were always big with worry. She took nerve pills, drank nerve tonic, visited with voodoo women in shacks near the bayou west of town. They made necklaces of teeth and chicken feet for her to wear. I once found her in the backyard throwing a kitchen chair into the air, letting it clunk down on her head. I watched her do it three times before she sat in the grass, her legs stretched out in front of her like a stiff doll's. She looked as if she had just woken up from a good night's sleep. The blood trickling down her neck confused her. When I finally walked over and put my hand on her shoulder, she jumped, made a noise like a bird.

This afternoon, after I fixed up the rockets, I went over to Durina's house. James's teal bubble of a rental car was parked out front, but no one was home. I looked in the drying shed, too, and no one was there. Then I found James's assistant du jour, lying in the grass on the side of the house, wearing only his underpants, swatting at the love bugs twisting in the air around his head. The kid must have been about sixteen, skinny, blond, all forced smiles.

"Hey," I said, "where'd everyone go?"

He sat up. "James and Durina went into town to discuss business."

"In what car?"

"James and I fought on the plane. He rented two cars so he wouldn't have to look at me."

"Nice guy," I said.

"I'm sick of his bullshit, anyway." The kid stood, stretched his skinny arms over his head. No hair in his armpits.

"Did James like Durina's shoes?"

"Loved them," the kid said. "She made some basic mules with this yellow alligator skin that were okay. Exotic preppy. I thought the other pairs totally sucked. I don't know why James got all worked up over them. I mean, when I looked at them, I thought they were what they were: some redneck's idea of fashion."

I hit the kid then. Punched his chest. He fell over. Made funny breathing noises. I think one of his ribs gave way when I punched it. Felt like that. He was so light. Empty. It was like punching a pillow set up on top of another pillow.

It's dark. The rockets look great. I replaced about twenty bulbs and all the necessary belts. They sound good, too. No squeaks. Smooth.

Officer Poimboeuf came by this afternoon, asked if I had my carnival ride permits in order and could he see them. I thought he came by to investigate my punching James's little nellie. Thought maybe I'd be busted for assault, so when he inquired about the permits for the rides, I was real polite and told him I had no intention of letting customers on until my permits were in order. Then I gave him some iced tea. When he sat down on my porch, I heard the crinkle of his diapers, and for a moment, I actually felt bad for him, wondered if there was a woman in this parish who didn't know about his diapers, a woman he could date for a while before breaking the news.

I could sit here in the moist grass and watch the rockets spin through the sky all night. Pet called. He wanted to come over, but I told him I'd be busy celebrating Durina's success.

The thing is, I know Durina won't be coming over.

Pageantry

Belinda's vintage Dior is itching her back. She's sick of this. The stink of hairspray and carnations, the buzzing lights, the color pink, all of it.

Ashleigh Borg, the new girl, taps Belinda on the knee and says, "I love your shoes."

"Thanks," Belinda says. "I love yours, too." Ashleigh is trash from Bowie. She wears a white dress—at least it's not pink—with puffy sleeves, something from an eighties prom. Her shoes are NineWest mall fare. She's nice enough, though. Belinda can almost believe her smile.

There are only seven girls in the Teen Miss category to-day. Last year, there were eleven. Four of them smartened up, and Belinda doesn't care that she'll never see them again. The entry fee is two hundred dollars for the Maryland Regionals. Each additional event category is twenty dollars. Prettiest Hair, Best Smile, Prettiest Eyes, Most Photogenic, Talent, Fashion Model, Personality Plus, and the High Point, which is a combination of events and almost always goes to Khristal Carr in Teen Miss. Khristal's the only one with parents dumb enough to pay for every extra event. Hardly any girls signed up for each category, so Khristal basically just bought her way into Nationals. She needed to. Belinda heard that the competition in Camden last week kicked Khristal's ass. Khristal was runner-up for Best Smile—nothing else.

The Miss Starlight pageant is run by a couple, Trina and Tony. Trina was on ESPN's *Body Shaping* years ago. Belinda has seen a tape. Another girl brought the tape to the Nationals last year. Drunk on 7-Up and stolen gin, Belinda and a few of the girls watched the tape in a small conference room in the hotel after flirting with a bellboy. The video showed Trina working out on a StairMaster in the background, grinning excruciatingly, wearing a pink-and-turquoise body suit. Trina won a few crowns back then, like Miss Simi Valley 1986 and Miss Orange Festival 1983. Before each pageant, Trina gives a pep talk to all the contestants. Belinda has noticed that Trina begins the pep talk in one of two ways: "When I was Miss Simi Valley . . ." or "Because I've been in pageantry for so many years . . ." Now Trina's too tan and her hair looks like hay. She has wrinkles that run perpendicular to her lips. She fills the crevices with makeup, but it doesn't hide them from Belinda, who has watched them become more pronounced over the years. Belinda wonders why Trina ever moved to the East Coast.

Belinda suspects that Trina's husband, Tony, is gay. He wears rings on each pinkie finger and knows a little too much about dresses and doing hair. At the end of each pageant, he hands out trophies and helps the girls with their tiaras. He has never once touched a girl inappropriately that Belinda has heard, and he's had a million chances. She once watched him check out Khristal's father, who, Belinda thinks, is actually pretty cute even though he dresses age-inappropriately in Abercrombie T-shirts and baggy jeans. Belinda wonders if Trina and Tony have an understanding; it might be okay that he's gay, and he may even have a live-in lover. Trina could be a lesbian, but Belinda thinks it's more likely that Trina suffered some sort of sexual trauma as a girl, and hasn't been interested in sex since. Their relationship is all about business, organizing these pageants, and cashing the checks written by stupid parents.

Every participant is presented with a trophy during the closing ceremony, even the girls who don't place in any event. Tiaras are available to purchase if a girl doesn't win one. Belinda has never had to buy a tiara. She always wins at least runner-up. Belinda has shelves of tiaras and trophies, and boxes of neatly folded sashes. When she was younger, she pretended her trophies were killer robots. She'd make them attack her Barbies. "No! Stop!" Barbie would yell, but the robots would keep marching. "Must kill Barbie. Must kill Barbie." The Barbies would always win the wars, but sometimes they'd lose Skipper or Ken in the battle. A Barbie was never killed, although more than once Belinda was tempted to let the trophy robots kill the African-American Barbie. She knew, even at age nine, that allowing African-American Barbie to be killed by the trophy robots could be construed as racist, but she was still tempted.

A few loud African-American teenagers had once yelled at her in Ralph Lauren. "Move your ass, cracker girl!" one demanded, pounding on the dressing-room door as Belinda was trying on a few skirts for school. Belinda's mother didn't say anything to the teenagers, who, Belinda thought, were going to beat her up—right there in Ralph Lauren, right next to a display of fluffy Shetland sweaters. She remained inside dressing room, coiled on the floor among tags and pins, crying silently into a tartan kilt, until her mother told her is was okay to come out, that the loud black girls had left.

"They're African-American girls," Belinda said through tears, "not *black* girls."

"Who's Freddy Krueger?" her mother asked her. "One of them called me Freddy Krueger."

"I don't know," Belinda had said. But she did know.

Belinda quit playing with Barbies after her uncle Derrick drew pubic hair and nipples on them with permanent marker. He had also molded a detailed penis for Ken from Silly Putty, and arranged the dolls in elaborate sexual tableaux for young Belinda to discover.

Winners in any category and runners-up in most are handed the White Packet along with the trophy, sash, and tiara. It's how Trina and Tony trap the parents into shelling out six hundred dollars for the Nationals, which this year are going to be held in Tampa. Belinda has told her mother several times that the Nationals are a gyp. "And besides," she added early this morning as they drove to the hotel in Timonium, "all the Teen Misses at the Nationals are sluts."

"They are not," her mother replied, tapping her fingers on the steering wheel.

"They walk like cowboys for a reason."

"Sometimes," Belinda's mother said, "you're just plain disgusting." She turned up the volume on the Volvo's stereo: the new Sting CD, which Belinda pretended to despise.

The White Packet contains all the registration papers and a glossy brochure for the resort that shows a waterslide and a big swimming pool. Last year, Belinda refused to swim after a lifeguard fished a tampon out of the deep end. Now she calls Tampa "Tampon." Tampon will be about a hundred degrees in August, and the girls' makeup will melt down their necks.

They conducted the Baby Miss pageant this morning, which is a relief for Belinda. She can't abide the squealing toddlers, especially while being stuck in this overheated conference hall under a thousand fluorescent lights, some of them strobing as they approach death. Whatever happened to lighting the stage only? But Belinda and the other Teen Misses still have to suffer through Mini Misses and Little Misses. Belinda sits there and smiles, pretends that all the little girls are cute. They're up there telling the judges that their favorite food is spaghetti and that they want to be astronauts when they grow up. Belinda knows their favorite food is Skittles and they'll all grow up to be slutty secretaries in Arlington or Bethesda—if they're not all mothers before junior high, strolling their malnourished brats through Towson Town Center, shoplifting from Baby Gap and Nordstrom.

Khristal has already had two abortions. Belinda knows a girl from Crofton who's in geometry with her.

There's no way Kristal would give up her career in pageantry to have a bunch of kids. There's no way she'll stop fucking, either, and because she's too stupid to make her zitty mullet-haired suitors wear condoms, she's got a punch card at Planned Parenthood.

Maybe it's a lie about Khristal, Belinda thinks. Khristal seems genuinely happy each time she's up there getting a trophy or a sash or a crown, carefully picking the blond strands of hair from the gooey corners of her surprised mouth. She's first to compliment other girls after they earnestly belt out some tired Whitney Houston song. And she is pretty. Belinda can't begrudge her that. Khristal's hair is naturally golden, and thick. Her eyes are big, but not buggish. And she has tits, real tits—not too big or too small. Somewhere between softballs and baseballs.

Belinda remembers that Khristal's been objectified since she was four months old, so she probably is a whore, and she might have even had that horrible operation in Mexico to get a few ribs removed. Belinda learned about the objectification of women last year in Mr. Moore's American Trends class. Belinda wrote a research paper on *Baywatch,* which Mr. Moore had called "brilliant and nearly groundbreaking."

Belinda reminds herself that not everyone is fortunate enough to attend the National Cathedral School like she is. Not everyone's parents can afford the 20K for tuition. So Khristal isn't a slut. She's just ignorant. Like the mean packs of African-American teenagers who shove their way down sidewalks in Georgetown.

There are only two Mini Misses in the Talent Category today. A pudgy redhead sings "I'm a Little Teapot," and a blond girl with a lazy eye sings "Twinkle, Twinkle, Little Star." The blond keeps singing, repeating one verse, won't surrender the microphone, apparently thinks she's cute in front of the adoring audience, who laugh and clap. Belinda scans the spectators for the little girl's mother, who, like most mothers here, has a fake'n'bake orange tan almost as bad as Trina's. Belinda wonders if the mothers look to Trina as a fashion role model. The singer's mother feigns embarrassment as her daughter performs. She covers her mouth with her plump, jeweled fingers, and crouches down as she fake-laughs. She most likely has coached her daughter into repeating the verse. Belinda imagines the little girl's mother's red face last night: "Don't forget. *Do not* forget. Keep singing. Wait for my signal." But, sorry, lady; it's been done a hundred times, and you should take your daughter to a real stylist. You shouldn't have done her hair yourself. If you patch her good eye, her lazy one will catch up. Your pediatrician should have told you that.

• • •

There are four Little Misses in the Fashion Model event: the same two from Talent, and two others. One of the others is standard, with generic bleached pageant hair, a soft face, cheap makeup, and a revealing retro outfit of go-go boots, vinyl miniskirt, and a tube top that looks more like a headband. Belinda can't help but roll her eyes when the girl climbs on stage. This outfit on a six-year-old. And the girl's squinting coyly and winking at the judges like she wants to fuck them. She faces the sparkling pink curtains at the back of the stage, spreads her skinny legs, leans over, face to knees, and smiles at the judges through her legs like a chick in Belinda's uncle's *Hustler* or *Penthouse* magazines. Belinda can see the little girl's future as clearly as she can see the little girl's panties.

The fourth girl is a mongrel, which is mean to think, Belinda knows, but she's honestly the ugliest thing Belinda has ever seen in eight years of pageantry. She has shapeless brown hair, wide-set Tori Spelling fish eyes, a flat nose, and teeth like a jack-o'-lantern. Her dress is from Factory 2 U or the back racks at Walmart. Belinda wishes she didn't know this. Shoes: white pumps from Payless, $7.99. Her inbred hillbilly mother is too stupid to take her to Ross or Marshalls and get her something okay for the same amount of money she squandered on that crap. Her mother

wasted two hundred dollars on the entry fee plus whatever for the Optional Events when Belinda's sure their
refrigerator and cupboards at home are empty except
for store-brand cheese singles and ramen noodles.

Belinda makes the depressing mistake of looking for
the mongrel's mother in the audience. The woman
meets Belinda's expectations. She's easy to spot in her
sky-blue sweatshirt, an eagle emblazoned across the
front, and black stirrup pants. The dumpy uniform of
fat ladies. The mother is actually crossing her fingers
and looks to be mumbling prayers, like she's invested
everything in her homely daughter, who's up on stage
twirling awkwardly in her plastic shoes. The poor
woman thinks her homely little daughter is her ticket
out of the shitty life she's leading. Belinda decides that
the noble thing to do would be to enlighten the
woman: Save your daughter from all this. Save your
money.

Khristal leans over to Belinda and says, "Is this girl
part retriever?"

"That's cruel," Belinda whispers, even though she's
thinking way crueler things. "What if someone said that
about you?"

"You're so right," Khristal says. "I feel so guilty."
For once, Khristal stops smiling and Belinda sees that
her face has no shape, no character, like a corn muffin.

From Belinda's other side, Ashleigh leans over and

says, "Are you guys talking about how ugly this chick is? She looks retarded."

"That's a pretty bitchy and bold thing to say, especially since this is your first pageant," Belinda tells her. "You could be disqualified for that remark."

Ashleigh shuts up, grins, watches the mongrel on stage pose for the judges.

The girl spins and curtseys like a trained chimp. Not even a vague sense of poise. Belinda imagines herself pulling the mother aside and whispering loudly: "Look, she's ugly as shit. Spend money on making her smart. Buy her a computer or something, because no dress, no shoes, and no talent will ever be good enough to eclipse her ugliness."

Then Belinda thinks maybe she should offer her old dresses to the woman. Belinda has a closet full of real pageant dresses, half of which, she thinks, would fit the little mongrel. And shoes. Good Shoes. Italian shoes. No plastic. Belinda looks up at the mongrel again, who's now standing on the edge of the stage, having finished her pathetic model strut and twirl. A little makeup. Something to give life to that hair. A real haircut. Braces and headgear. But it's no use; the girl is ugly, and Belinda feels it in her stomach.

Nothing sucks more than this waiting. Sitting stiffly on the metal folding chairs, face aching from smiling, watching these little girls transform into whores, one after the other. At least, Belinda decides, the mongrel is too ugly to become a whore—although, Belinda has learned that there are some pretty desperate guys. Half of the guys at St. Albans, all from Washington's best families, would fuck a goat if given the chance.

Belinda's mother was burned when she was fifteen, Belinda's age. Belinda's uncle Derrick filled a plastic baggie with gasoline and taped a few bottle rockets to it. The bag was tied to three helium balloons. He made a slow-burning wick from a cigarette. There was supposed to be a huge explosion high in the sky over Washington, an explosion that no one could ever explain, an event that would stump experts for years to come.

The gas–bottle-rocket–balloon setup was too heavy, and the bomb just hovered and bobbed next to Belinda's mother's bedroom window, blocked from its slow ascent by branches from a tree that still stands there despite being scorched.

The bomb finally exploded right as her mother leaned out her window to ask Derrick what it was.

Derrick was twenty-seven at the time.

Now the right side of her mom's face is ruined. *Ruined* is the word Belinda thinks and says. "No details," Belinda tells her friends when they ask. "Just know that she's not pretending to be famous when she wears sunglasses and a lot of scarves and Pashminas." Her friends understand. They don't give her shit about the pageants. A few have even come to pageants. None of them is here today.

Only Belinda will admit that Uncle Derrick is mentally challenged, developmentally disabled. He still lives with Belinda's grandparents in Chevy Chase and works at White Flint Mall—in the back of Sharper Image, opening boxes with razors, which Belinda thinks is dangerous. He gleefully tells Belinda the story of the day he ruined her mom's face whenever he can. He still gets excited when he talks about people reporting the balloon bomb as a UFO, how the Pentagon and the Air Force would have gotten involved. "That damn tree! That fuck tree! Fuck tree! It would have been in *Time* magazine!"

Belinda sits here, grins, wonders about her makeup, shows off the fine and expensive work of her orthodontist, counts the days until she turns eighteen and no longer qualifies for this third-rate pageant organization. Exactly 1,039 days until her eighteenth birthday. Belinda sits here for her mother, who was once called "Crispy Face" by a drunk man on Wisconsin Avenue.

Belinda knows she could never make it in a real pageant like Miss America or Miss USA. She's too smart, and she's too short—only five-three. At least her tits are proportional to the rest of her. She's not one of those short chicks with huge tits who have to get breast reduction surgery to save their spines.

Belinda's father was short and smart, according to Belinda's mother. At the time he donated, he was a law student. He had an I.Q. of 147. Like Belinda's mother, he was of Irish and Welsh descent. He stood five-six with light brown hair. His interests were fishing, sailing, and jazz.

Belinda imagines that some day she'll find him. He'll be walking down near the Capitol, wearing an expensive suit and shoes, talking on a cell phone. Every short man she sees down there could be him. Her mother won't talk about him anymore, but Belinda has convinced herself that he stayed in D.C. after law school. She refuses to believe that he may have gone to law school in any another city, that maybe he was just working in Washington between semesters.

In the summer, Belinda takes the Metro into the city. She sits on the white cool steps of the Capitol and watches for short men while the sun freckles her arms. She sips on lemonade that she buys from a vendor in front of the Natural History Museum. On any given afternoon, twenty short men, nicely dressed, walk past her, their leather-soled shoes make the right noise on the steps, and she thinks any one of them could be her father.

She followed a man once. He wore linen trousers, pleated because he had muscular legs—Belinda could tell from his tight butt. A white shirt. No tie. His hair was cut short and it was the same color as Belinda's: light brown, like mouse fur. But his nose is what made Belinda follow him. It was a bigger version of Belinda's, exactly: slightly hooked, with a thin bridge and a shadow of a dimple.

He walked quickly down the Capitol steps, weaving through tourists and panhandlers like he was late for an important meeting or had to pee. Belinda could barely keep up in the muggy heat, cursed herself for wearing mules, pushed through a crowd of students gathered around a Krishna booth. She felt the fluttering excitement in her stomach when she caught up to him in the cool Metro tunnel. She was relieved to see he wasn't jogging down the escalator; he was casually riding it.

She tried not to look at him on the Metro, but she couldn't help it. She imagined him as a law student, carefully considering the ramifications of donating sperm. Did he do it for the money? Or did he do it because he felt it was his duty to pass on his genes? She wondered if she had any half-siblings, how many children he had fathered. Did he ever think about running into his children on the street? If he proved to be her father, would he take her fishing on the Chesapeake? Or to secret, smoky jazz clubs under the bridge on K Street? He was handsome in his basic clothes.

She followed him to the student center at George Washington University, and thought that he must be a law professor. He read the *Post* at a table overlooking a cement courtyard, which was empty except for a woman collecting cans from a trash bin.

When another man, taller with a head of blond curls, kissed the man Belinda suspected was her father, kissed him fully on the mouth, Belinda ran from the student center, nearly losing a mule on the escalator leading into the subway tunnel.

It wasn't until she reached Chevy Chase that she realized that a gay man could have donated sperm.

"My friends and I ride the Metro to the monuments and Smithsonian museums whenever we can," Belinda lies to a judge. The judge is an older version of Tony. Belinda wonders if he knows the man she followed, but then catches herself in the bigoted assumption that all gay men know each other.

"What else do you do for fun?" he asks.

She would love to tell him the truth: *We get drunk and try on Prada, or we take acid and get someone to drive us around all night.* But she doesn't. Instead, she tells him that she's very involved in sports: soccer, tennis, field hockey, and she volunteers at a soup kitchen.

The next judge, an older woman with stretched earlobes, whom Belinda recognizes from other pageants, asks Belinda what her goals are.

"I'd like to be a microbiologist," Belinda says through her smile. "I'd like to develop antibiotics as quickly as bacteria mutates."

The woman looks confused, which is good, except that Belinda fears the woman remembers the Northern Virginia Regionals four months ago, when Belinda answered that she'd like to be a physicist when she grows up, because, she had explained, perpetual-motion machines could save the planet.

Belinda looks to her mother, who's sitting next to Khristal's parents. Her mother waves with her fingers and adjusts her scarf. Maybe, if Belinda argues just right, and if she doesn't see that sadness wash across the good side of her mother's face, she'll only have to go to Tampon one more time. Maybe she can hang up her dresses for good, box her tiaras and trophies, never have to see Trina and Tony again. What is it, though? About ten days out of the year: a day to prepare for the pageant, the pageant, a day or two to prepare for Tampon, five days in Tampon . . .

Trina walks on stage. Belinda has seen her dress before. Blocks of red, yellow, and blue, like the uniform the girls at Hot-Dog-on-a-Stick wear, like a Mondrian painting. Belinda remembers the oral report she gave on Mondrian last year: *Mondrian crashed through the convention of three-dimensional space and curves* . . . She wonders how many people in the room know who Mondrian was. She wonders how many have ever been to an art museum.

As Trina announces the Mini Miss winners, as mothers scream and cheer, as little girls cry, as others jump and clap and smile, Belinda recalls more of the Mondrian report: . . . *which he moved around the canvas until he found the perfect composition* . . . She had actually hated General Art History, but studied enough, spending hours in the slide library, to earn an A-.

"Are you nervous?" Khristal asks Belinda. "I am."

"Why?"

"You didn't hear?" Khristal whispers.

"No," Belinda says. "I didn't."

"I didn't get a packet in Camden."

Belinda doesn't respond. There are only seven Teen Misses today. If Khristal needs to get herself worked up, if she needs this false sense of excitement, of desperation, she'll let her have it.

When Belinda sees the mongrel up on stage receiving a trophy and White Packet for Best Smile, she clenches her teeth. The mongrel's mother is crying, bouncing in her seat, snapping photos with a disposable camera. It'll cost the mongrel and her mother at least a thousand dollars to get down to Tampon and enter in the Nationals. The mongrel stands at the front of the stage and waves to no one, grins widely, until Tony ushers her away.

A few minutes later, Belinda wins First Runner Up Miss Teen Starlight. She doesn't fake a smile as she steps on stage. She doesn't thank Tony as he crowns her. She moves off the stage before Trina announces Miss Teen Starlight Maryland, Khristal. Belinda doesn't look at her mother. She doesn't look at the mongrel's mother. She pushes through girls, into the hall, where she sits on the patterned carpeting next to a Coke machine, until she realizes that going back in and smiling is the best thing to do.

A Note on the Type

The text of this book was set in Wayland, a mysteriously misnamed typeface designed in 1949 by an Urg Kis, a Hungarian immigrant who lived quietly with his wife and children in Medford, Massachusetts.

Simon's Aunt Lena had inherited the house, a three-story mansion with a capacious gusty attic and a dirt-floored cellar, because several generations of the family—the Kis family—knew that she couldn't survive anywhere else. It had been Simon's great-grandparents' house, then his grand-parents', the house where his father and Aunt Lena grew up. Now it was Aunt Lena's house.

From Simon's father's old photos and stories, Simon knew Aunt Lena had always been ugly. She looked to him like a pirate, like Captain Hook from Disney's *Peter Pan*. Her chin jutted, and her left eye was in a constant squint. Her eyebrows were woolly like her father's, whose own eyebrows grew ferociously and sometimes impaired his vision. She had bulky forearms, and knuckles like a meat packer's.

Simon's father told him that the neighborhood kids used to call Lena "Man-Girl" and say she had been born with a penis, a penis that was lost in a circumcision accident. The teasing was cruel and must have stung, but the penis rumor, Simon thought, may have been valid. Lena was clearly suffering from a genetic mixup or hormonal imbalance.

Her parents took her out of school when her mustache began to push through her upper lip at the onset of puberty. She was tutored by her grandfather—Simon's great-grandfather—Urg, a famous and wealthy type designer who, late in life, out of boredom—or so his family thought—earned a teaching certificate at the teachers' college in Salem. He tutored a few other troubled wealthy children, molded them into responsible scholars who went on to take advantage of their families' long-standing relationships with colleges and universities throughout New England.

According to Simon's father, Lena's tutelage had been on the up-and-up scholastically, perhaps more intellectually challenging than any school, public or private. But after living with his aunt for the summer, Simon concluded she would have been much better off venturing out of the house and attending school with other girls her own age. She would have been better off if she had learned to abide adolescent cruelties. Even the freakiest misfits in Simon's high school had made friends. Some even had sex. All of them learned the most basic forms of human interaction. Aunt Lena never had.

Because of this, Simon's summer in Medford, the Boston suburb where his aunt lived, was marked by countless uncomfortable moments. Simon was headed to veterinary school that fall, at the university just down the road from his aunt's house. But he had no love for animals. He never had. It was jealousy that led him to veterinary school, profound and blatant jealousy of his younger brother, Brian, who wanted desperately to be a vet but didn't have the grades or the standardized-test scores to be admitted to even the most questionable vet schools in the Caribbean. Brian had tried. Poor cretin. Simon had both the grades and the scores, and the sickening ability to feign a passion for anything— even helping animals. He spent an hour doing just that for the admissions committee, expressing a need to return to his parents' time-share beach house in San Carlos, Mexico, after finishing vet school, to neuter all the semi-feral strays that scampered through the town in search of handouts from bleeding-heart gringos. Simon worked it. He let the tears stream down his face when he spoke of a particularly mangy bitch who had begged a burrito and taken it behind a Dumpster to feed her emaciated puppies. The committee lapped it up, a few cried themselves, and several months later, there he was: back in Medford, skulking around his aunt's mansion, peeking in places better left unpeeked, learning about his family.

Aunt Lena didn't speak much, but Simon knew almost instantly that his presence in her house—her world, really—was intrusive and unwelcome. She twitched when he first hugged her. And during the first few minutes in her house, as he was lugging his suitcases up the creaking staircase, she fixed him with her cold stare, squinted both eyes, and audibly ground her teeth.

A one-bedroom apartment in the Medford-Somerville-Cambridge area went for at least eight hundred a month. It would have been foolish for him to live anywhere other than with Lena: share a shack with some foreign grad students, squat in a gutted-out row house with anarchists, play pious and live in a Christian co-op—he had already endured too many ridiculous domestic situations, lost too many deposit checks, and he thought it was about time he sponged off a relative.

Simon chose a bedroom on the second floor with eastern light. Lena slept up on the third, on the west end. His bed, a king-size four-poster, ornately carved to resemble Native American totem poles, was thick with dust. The room smelled like the white safety paste they used to give to him in elementary-school art class.

As he was placing his socks in the dresser, he discovered a shoe box, an L.L. Bean moccasin box from the fifties or sixties, in the bottom drawer. He closed the door to his new room, placed the box on his bed, and opened it. In pink and green cellophane Easter grass nested a large wooden dildo, detailed with veins and a rolled back foreskin. It was carved from a dark wood, perhaps mahogany, polished and shellacked, much like the bedposts, and at first he had thought it must have come from the bed, from one of the totems. But he looked up and down each post and found no possible origin: each totem was intact, and none looked big enough to sport such a huge genital.

He neatly placed his socks in the drawer next to the box, reassured by the cobwebs enshrouding the dildo that his aunt would not be looking for it anytime soon, that his family's prurience was something of the past.

That night, staring into the water stains on the ceiling, breathing in the fumes of his new surroundings, he figured that at least twenty percent of the homes in the United States contained a hidden dildo. Maybe more than twenty percent. It could have been Aunt Lena's or his grandmother's, or maybe an aunt's or cousin's who had once stayed in the mansion. He knew that his grandparents employed maids and other servants for a brief period when his father and Lena were children, and certainly one of them could have been lonely and horny enough to own a dildo. He preferred to think that it had been a horny maid's dildo. He resigned himself to think that it had been a horny maid's dildo.

The matrices became the property of the Wayland Foundry in 1950, and Kis was not credited with the design until 1963, thirty-seven years after his death.

After Simon finished up in the bathroom that first morning, he walked downstairs to get some breakfast, hoping to begin a nephew-aunt relationship with some pleasant morning conversation.

Aunt Lena sat in the breakfast nook, reading a romance magazine, crunching through a bowl of corn flakes, milk slipping over her chin, down her neck, into her shirt. She didn't move her eyes from her magazine when Simon entered the kitchen.

"This house is huge," Simon said to her from across the room. "I'm still finding my way around." That was true. He had spent a good portion of the morning searching the mansion for toilet paper. He forced a smile.

She finally looked up from her magazine, her dark eyes partially obscured by the thickness of her eyebrows, her left eye screwed into its tight squint. "If you need anything, just ask," she cracked after a deep breath.

"Thanks," he said.

"Don't be snooping around," she said, louder. "Don't be looking through all the bathrooms!"

"I was just—"

"Don't do it!" she screamed, and she flung the magazine in his direction. It slapped the floor and slid across the linoleum, stopping at his bare, bony feet: LOVE CAN HAPPEN! HE WAS MORE THAN A SEX SLAVE! THE WARM HANDS OF HER SURGEON . . .

He was frightened by her outburst and quickly retreated to his bedroom, sat on his bed, and stared at the dresser while the adrenaline drained from his stomach. He hadn't thought that looking for toilet tissue would be a problem. He decided to let Aunt Lena cool down. He'd find breakfast elsewhere, maybe in Medford Square. He'd buy her a small gift, just a card or something, and apologize for his intrusive toilet-paper hunt. He'd also buy some toilet paper.

When he went for his socks he noticed the dildo box was gone. Only socks. His system flushed with adrenaline again. He was overcome with heartburn and esophageal reflux and fast shallow breathing. He sat on the floor, one hand clutching his chest.

It bothered him to think that Lena's thick fingers were rifling through his socks. More troubling, though, was the fact that Lena knew he knew about the dildo. She was probably hoping that he had never opened the box, that he had just seen it there and let it be—a box in a drawer was none of his business, right? Why would he open it?

Had she sneaked into his bedroom as he slept and retrieved the dildo? He imagined her, tiptoeing as daintily as someone husky as she could tiptoe, finding the dildo safe in its box. She picked off the cobwebs, sighed deeply, and held it against her pocked cheek. Maybe she paused at Simon's bed, looked down at him, his thin arms—arms he'd work on bulking up this summer—crossed over his chest like a mummy's, and brushed the hair from his forehead.

Or worse.

• • •

It is an old-style book face of excellent clarity and sharpness, much like Kis's Swartmight book face, which brought him fame among publishers on both sides of the Atlantic.

"I'm telling you, Aunt Lena hates me already." Simon had called his mother in Oregon from a pay phone in the lobby of the Medford Public Library.

"She does not," his mother said. "She's just not used to having people around."

"She yelled at me."

"I doubt it," she said. "You'll feel more settled when classes start in the fall."

"I found a dildo in the dresser in my room."

A weak sigh. "You didn't touch it, did you?"

"Of course not."

Another weak sigh. "Brian got some wonderful news yesterday."

Simon hated how his mother didn't use segues when it came to praising his brother. "What now?" he asked.

"When you come home for the holidays, turn to channel twelve at six o'clock and you'll see him doing the weather. He looks so handsome in a suit, and they're paying him more than—"

Simon hung up.

He stared at the back of his hand gripping the receiver, noticed the scar from his ganglion cyst removal, examined his knuckles. His hand looked old, veined, and weathered, like his grandfather's hand, though he was only twenty-eight.

Simon returned to Lena's a few hours later, carrying an eight-pack of toilet paper, and the embarrassingly maudlin gift he chose for her: a small teddy bear wearing a T-shirt that read, I'M BEARY SORRY. He left the teddy bear on the table in the breakfast nook beside a stack of romance magazines.

For the rest of the day, Aunt Lena avoided him. Each time they came close to one another, he felt as if he had interrupted something private, like prayer or masturbation. She'd emit a feeble guttural chirp, scurry off, and hide up in her bedroom.

He busied himself in his own room, unpacking, reading through the vast paperwork from vet school. The day ached on. When he ventured down to the kitchen late in the afternoon, he did notice the teddy bear was gone. He also noticed that there was nothing to eat except four different brands of corn flakes. To drink: soy milk, or tap water. Most of the cupboards were packed with romance magazines, some as old as forty years. The refrigerator held only the soy milk, seven cartons. The boxes of corn flakes were lined up on the counter like a set of encyclopedias. Next to the refrigerator was the door to the basement steps. Simon opened that door, thinking maybe it was a walk-in cupboard, and was greeted by a rush of cool, fresh air.

"Shut that!" Aunt Lena yelled at him from somewhere across the house.

Simon felt her words in his stomach, nearly lost the little food he had eaten in Medford Square. "I was just—"

"Shut it!"

Wayland serifs are concave and splayed; the contrast between thick and thin strokes is marked, dramatic.

The supermarket closest to Lena's house, the only one within walking distance, was a bag-your-own-groceries-and-buy-in-bulk-to-save-a-few-cents type. Busted shopping carts filled the drainage ditch next to the parking lot, and open packages of cereal and powdered milk littered the floors inside. Shrill screams of hungry, bored children and their impatient mothers shot down the aisles.

He chose a loaf of wheat bread, one that hadn't been squashed, and headed to the deli counter, where he promptly took a number and began to examine the meats and other foods behind the smudged glass: gelatin and whipped-cream salads, sliced roast beef glazed with rainbow oil slicks, tubs of pickles and orange macaroni. The deli counter was staffed by a fat older man in a Red Sox cap who breathed heavily as he weighed potato salad, and a thirtyish woman who looked as if she had never grown out of her high-school partying phase. Simon looked at her name tag: CHARLENE.

Charlene's face was hard, and the hair hanging from her crusty corduroy ball cap was perfectly feathered. He imagined her, age twelve, losing her virginity in the back of a Ford Pinto wagon, bad pot and Jack Daniel's mixing with the stink of impending sex, her suitor's hair longer than hers, his bony chest beading with sweat as he tried to unlace her jeans . . . But then Simon thought maybe her whole look was some ironic retro-retro-early-eighties thing, that she was a White Trash Theorist, a graduate student who'd designed her own major at one of the area's prestigious universities. Maybe her job at the deli counter was just a way of gathering ethnographic data for her dissertation: *Power Trash and Cracker Culture*. She became cool and brilliant and fashionable in his mind, someone he had to get to know, someone who might appreciate the creepiness of his Aunt Lena.

Simon was delighted when Charlene, not the old fat man, called his number, twenty-four, in her heavy, probably affected, Medford accent: twenny fo-ah.

"One pound of the low-salt turkey, please," he said, wondering if her coworker at the deli was the subject of her study. "Extremely thin slices." He smiled hard. The images of her first sexual encounter raced through his brain again. He adjusted the front of his trousers.

She began to reach her gloved hand into a plastic tub of presliced turkey.

He stopped her. "I was hoping you could slice it fresh for me," he said, pointing to the slicers on the counter behind her.

She held up a wad of turkey slices. "This was sliced, like, an hour ago." She rolled her eyes away from his, tapped her sneakered foot.

"I'd rather it be sliced now, thank you," he said.

"Tough shit," she said.

"Excuse me?"

"Tough shit." She began to pile the presliced turkey onto to the scale.

"What's your manager's name?"

She continued with the piling, humming until she looked up and said, "His name's Frank. I'll call him back here if you want." She ripped one slice in two and stacked the smaller piece on the scale, making the pile a perfect sixteen ounces. "Anything else?"

"No," he said. "Thank you, Charlene."

He had been wrong about her intellect. She was not the brilliant social critic he had imagined. She was just what she appeared to be. Dim. Ravaged. Grumpy. Overwrought. Stuck. Raised on fast food and bad television.

He shopped around for a few minutes, grabbed a jar of Dijon mustard, a few overripe tomatoes, a head of browning lettuce, and hustled back to the deli for some Swiss. The other customers had cleared.

"Excuse me," Simon said to Charlene, as she drained cloudy liquid from a vat of beige-colored sausages, "may I have a half of a pound of Swiss, please?"

Charlene ignored him, tipped the vat a little more. A few slick sausages plopped onto the floor. She kicked them under the sink with her grimy sneaker. They glided nicely.

"Excuse me," he said.

She turned around. "I guess you didn't see the twenty or thirty signs that say take a number," she said. And she went right back to draining the milky liquid from the sausage vat.

"Why should I take a number if I'm the only one here?"

The fat guy walked out, picked his ear, looked at his finger. "What do you need?" he said to Simon.

"I was talking to the young woman," he said. "We were discussing this take-a-number business."

"You're supposed to take a number," the man said. "See the signs?"

"Of course I see the signs, but I'm the only customer at the counter now."

"We're not authorized to help you unless you take a number," he said.

Simon settled on prepackaged low-fat Swiss.

● ● ●

The italic is rather eccentric, but not hard on the eye.

Those first few weeks in Medford flew by. Simon quickly realized that he'd get no pity from his mother back at home—she was too busy fawning over his TV-star brother. When Simon told his father about Lena, his father dismissed him as cruel. "I thought you could help my sister," he said. "I never expected you'd act like all those kids I used to have to beat up." When Simon called his friends and complained, they all posed the same rhetorical question: "Do you know how much I'm paying for rent?"

Simon decided that he could easily abide Aunt Lena in order to save eight hundred dollars per month. Once his financial aid package kicked in, he'd be living large. He already knew what he'd tell the other students at vet school: "I'm taking care of a developmentally disabled relative, a cousin three times removed." That would really only be a half-lie. If any new friends visited him at Lena's, they'd see he had a sweet deal, and they'd certainly believe Lena was mentally retarded.

Simon's living pattern developed quickly.

He'd play on the Internet until two or three in the morning, eat breakfast at noon, try to get out of the house before one, explore the greater Medford area until supper, which he ate around seven. His schedule allowed minimal contact with Lena. That third week, he only saw her four times—he kept track—and only nine words were exchanged between them: what-time-does-the-mail-come-I-don't-know.

He soon learned, however, that Medford Square, with its fast food and card shops, was no place to kill time. Neither was West Medford Square. He was accosted there by three teenage girls, the second of whom, shaking her spiral perm and giant hoop earrings, threatened to kick his pansy ass if he ever dared look at her friend again. The university was no relief because Simon couldn't use its facilities until the fall, when he would be an official student.

The Medford Public Library teemed with the usual deviants and lunatics. He spent too many afternoons sitting across a reading table from an old man who wasted sheet after sheet of paper drawing dinosaurs with a red pen. When they started the noisy and dusty task of refurbishing the periodicals room in early July, Simon vowed never to return. And he didn't.

Simon began to spend his afternoons at the Davis Municipal Swimming Pool instead, swimming laps and sunbathing with the rest of Medford. He often shared a lane with three other swimmers, the four of them swimming in circles, constantly passing one another, kicking and scratching, pausing at the ends in exasperated frustration. The pool had only four kickboards for public use, and two of them had what looked to be large bites taken from them.

There was a kid there at the pool whom Simon dubbed "Little Asshole" in his mind the first time he observed him. Little Asshole lipped off to the lifeguards and refused to leave the pool area when asked. He continued to be an asshole, and whenever Simon was lucky enough to get a kickboard those first few weeks, he could see what Little Asshole was up to. Usually the kid was harassing young women, sizing up their breasts and asses, grabbing his penis through his bathing suit and twisting it like a bored caged monkey might do, or else ferociously scratching at his arms and legs, making Simon wonder whether the chlorine level was too high. Little Asshole was about thirteen or fourteen, a dirty smear of a mustache on his upper lip, a gawky posture, shaggy hair, pimpled back. The lifeguards hated him, but they were faced with him every day. They'd constantly blow their whistles and yell his awful real name: Stevie!

Simon soon learned that Charlene the deli clerk was Little Asshole's mother, and he wasn't at all surprised. He had imagined Stevie's parents before, and he imagined Stevie's conception to be much like what he had imagined Charlene's deflowering to be.

Charlene showed up the afternoon two of the buff male lifeguards had detained Stevie in the office to stop him from biting another dorkish pubescent boy. Charlene was wearing the cap and meat-stained apron she wore at work. She appeared to be as tired as ever, with bruised-looking eyes and an unlit cigarette hanging limply from her mouth. Two other cigarettes were tucked behind her ears.

Charlene pulled Stevie by his hair from the pool area. When they passed his lane, Simon glanced up from his kickboard and said, "Hello." Charlene looked at him confusedly and continued to tug screeching Stevie.

• • •

Old Face traditions are neither completely ignored nor completely heeded.

Simon's mother called him periodically to report on his brother's progress as weatherman. "You have to see the suits they bought him, Simon. They're beautiful," she said, the last time he let her talk about him.

Simon said, "I bet."

After Simon's brother had arrived at the television station, they fired the old weatherman—a bald slob with a pathetic comb-over—and gave his brother both the six and the ten o'clock slots. "And you wouldn't believe what they're paying him."

"Oh, boy," Simon said.

"I thought you let go of that jealousy a long time ago, Simon."

"I'm not jealous," he said. "I'm bored. Remarkably bored."

"Only boring people get bored," she said.

"Really? I thought only boring mothers bored nonboring sons with boring updates of their other, boring son."

"Jealousy is one of the strongest and most basic emotions."

"Spare me."

"Even dogs get jealous. You'll learn that in vet school."

"May I please hang up now?" Simon said.

"That's rude."

"I can't think of a more polite way of asking that question."

"The notion is rude, not the phrasing." She hung up then.

The first book to be printed in the Wayland type was *Unsung Heroes of American Industry* by Mark Jude Poirier, published in 1957 in nearby Sudbury by the short-lived Farnham Press.

Simon learned Charlene's shift schedule, and he walked to the supermarket every other day, ordered a half pound of low-salt turkey. When his number was called by one of the other deli clerks—the fat man he saw the first time, an older woman whose gaudy rings ripped through her rubber gloves, or an anabolic kid who looked like a defensive lineman—he politely said, "I prefer Charlene to wait on me."

In late July, he decided to introduce himself: "I'll have the usual, please, Charlene."

She curled her upper lip. "What's the usual?"

"A half a pound of low-salt turkey," Simon said. He smiled weakly. "My name's Simon, by the way."

She sighed and stacked the presliced turkey on the scale.

Simon's mind spun as he inhaled the smells of the deli counter. He watched her closely. She favored her right leg a little, her hips cocked to the left. Maybe she had fallen off a motorcycle. Been kicked by a drunk heavy-metal freak at a Motörhead concert. Stabbed by one of her trashy girlfriends—the result of an argument over a spilled bong. Or maybe Stevie had thuked her kneecap with an aluminum bat during one of his rages.

She handed Simon his meat.

"I see you at the pool sometimes," Simon said. "When Stevie's in trouble."

"Next," she said, looking over Simon's head. "Number thirty-six."

Farnham Press published several more poorly received books in the Wayland typeface, including Martha Weston's *A Woman's Guide to Mining Careers* and Parker Jefferson's *All Roads Lead to Love,* which sold fewer than one hundred copies each.

• • •

Simon was interrupted by Lena as he ate his second turkey and Swiss sandwich one hot afternoon. He had arranged the wheat crumbs into a rhombus on the Formica table, and was staring vacantly at the rhombus, chewing, sweat tracing down his back, when Lena appeared, swinging open the door that led to the basement stairway.

"Hi," Simon said, through a mouthful of sandwich. "What's going on in the basement?"

Lena slammed the door and walked across the kitchen to Simon. She leaned her thick arms on the table in front of him. "Cleanliness," she said, "is absolutely necessary." She smelled gamey. Reminded Simon of the way his Scout Master smelled after three days of camping on Mount Hood. "As is respect for privacy."

"I agree," Simon said. "One hundred percent."

"Good then," Lena said. Simon thought he saw her mouth work itself into a vague hint of a smile. She grabbed a romance magazine from the countertop and marched out of the room.

Simon wondered what she was implying. He kept his room tidy and always washed and put away his dishes. As for respecting her privacy, he hadn't looked in any closets or cupboards since the toilet-paper hunt, he hadn't been down in the cellar, and he had practically forgotten about the dildo—until now.

Late that night, the electric fan propped in the open window offered no relief from the heat. Simon had masturbated in the shower earlier that evening, but he nonetheless found himself with an erection so strong it ached, making sleep in the heat even less likely.

He pulled on a pair of shorts and a T-shirt and walked barefoot down the stairs, clutching his rubber flip-flops under his arm, carefully placing each step so the planks wouldn't creak. He stepped out the back door into the humid night.

He knew Charlene wouldn't be working, but he walked to the supermarket anyway. There was nowhere else to go. An older woman whom Simon didn't recognize worked the deli counter. Simon didn't have to take a number. She smiled and asked him what he'd like.

"Oh, Charlene Vaccarino isn't working tonight?"

"No one named Charlene Vaccarino works here."

"What is Charlene's last name?" Simon asked. "I could have sworn it was Vaccarino."

The woman stripped off her rubber gloves. "Look," she said, "I can't tell you her last name. You could be a pervert. You could have a plastic rubbish bin full of chopped-off arms and legs in your cellar."

Simon thought for a moment. "I'm not a pervert," he said, looking through the glass at a glistening keg-sized loaf of head cheese. "And I don't have anything like that in my basement."

"Why are you here at two in the morning trying to get Charlene's last name?" she asked. "I should call the police."

"I know her," Simon said. "And I know her son Stevie from the pool."

"Then why don't you know her last name?"

"I said I thought it was Vaccarino."

"You're an awful liar," the woman said. "The pitch of your voice rises and you look away when you lie."

Had he lost his ability to lie? Surely if he could fool the admissions committee at the nation's best school of veterinary science, he could fool this meat-slicing drool.

"To prove I know her and Stevie," Simon said, staring intently into the woman's sunken gray eyes, "I'll leave her a note. Do you have a pen and a scrap of paper?"

The woman handed him a marking pen and ripped a large piece of butcher paper from the roll at the end of the counter.

All Simon could think of writing was: Hello, Charlene: I was here at the deli tonight and I thought I should say hello. I'll see you later this week. Say hello to Stevie, too.—Franklin

The woman looked over the short note written on the corner of the large sheet. "Your name isn't Franklin," she said. "Let's see some I.D."

"I won't even dignify that with a response, let alone by taking out my driver's license."

Simon walked away. He heard the woman mumble "pervert."

A teenage boy was working the only register open at that time of the night. He smiled hard and danced from one foot to the other. Fiddled with his belt loops. Scratched his elbows. The kid was hopped up on something, Simon figured. Simon asked him: "You know Charlene who works the deli counter in the afternoons? What's her last name?"

"We used to party with her and now we party with her son Stevie, which is weird, don't you think?" the kid said. He blew his blond bangs from his eyes with two quick puffs. "We don't talk about it with Stevie though because that would be weird for him knowing that. Don't you think that would be weird knowing that? That your mother used to party with your friends? With the guys you party with now? Don't you think?"

"Yes," Simon said when the kid finally paused. "What's Charlene's last name?"

"Her last name's Cartwright like on the cowboy show but Stevie's is something different because he got his dad's name which is something like Bacardi or Zanetti or Tinogamo or Morovatti. Something really Italian like that."

The pages of the phone book in the ratty booth outside the supermarket were water-damaged and stuck together, and Simon could barely work his fingers, but he found the listing for Cartwright—the only one in Medford, and right there on High Street. Seeing her name in print like that, seeing her address and phone number, gave Simon a sudden rush of libido, and he found himself rubbing up against the dirty Plexiglas before he caught his breath and ripped the page from the phone book.

He must have passed it a million times: 112 High Street, Medford, 02155.

The typeface lived on and became quite popular despite the failure of the books and the eventual closing of Farnham Press.

Simon didn't know what was driving him, causing him to place each step toward Charlene's house faster and faster until he was running, his flip-flops slapping the sidewalk; panting, feeling the atavistic urge in his teeth, his fingertips, his prick. Downtrodden, spent, tired Charlene. Grumpy and rude and uneducated. Mother of Stevie. Probably smelled like the deli, like cheese and nitrate-soaked meat.

Simon felt disgusting. He was a pervert. A Peeping Tom. Bound for prison.

The sweat stung his eyes. He could barely breathe. It seemed as if nothing made it into his lungs. The air was wet, thick, and hot. The weak breeze carried the polluted stench of the Mystic River, which Simon began to taste.

When he reached 112 High Street, he took a deep breath and turned off his mind like he'd take off an itchy sweater. Gone were the feelings of guilt, and the fear, and the racing thoughts of his mother weeping, newspaper articles, a self-righteous judge, horny and husky cellmates, his brother's smirk.

He couldn't see into her house, even up close, even with his nose and wet hands pressed against the window. She was upstairs now, in bed, he knew, probably in a T-shirt and panties. Cotton panties with a few holes, a stain, a loosening elastic. Her hair was sweat-soaked, and strewn over her pillow like a tangle of washed-up kelp. Prickly legs, not shaved in almost a week. Simon imagined her as clearly as if he had broken in and shined a flashlight across her bed.

Simon didn't remember climbing into Charlene's car, sprawling over the backseat, nuzzling into the sticky vinyl, so when Stevie and his buddies opened the car door, he felt as if he had woken from a weird fever dream.

It was still dark when they pulled him out of the car by his legs, his shorts down around his ankles, one flip-flop gone. He felt four or five hands, fingernails digging into his skin. He couldn't make out any of their faces, but he knew it was Stevie and his friends: he could hear

Stevie, smell the chlorine and sweat on Stevie's body. He kicked and squirmed and yelled, but the boys got a few good punches in, and tugged him onto the concrete. Simon's head thunked the ground. The boys began to kick and spit.

"Fucking pervert!" one of them yelled.

"Fag!" Stevie said.

"We'll kick your fucking ass!"

Simon acted crazy, grunted, drooled, flailed his arms, grabbed at his exposed penis.

"What the fuck?" Stevie said. "I think he's retarded or something."

"Or he's from Dorchester."

"My mom's from Dorchester, asshole."

They finally let Simon up, yelling "Tard!" at him as he wobbled down the sidewalk, only one flip-flop slapping the cement.

It was only through fate and delicate research that the Wayland font was proven to be the original work of Urg Kis, not Jessup Wayland II, the foundry's owner.

Simon saw Lena's silhouette in the window of her bedroom. Her chin's shadow was stretched across the drawn shade. She was awake. Probably doing something weird. Practicing witchcraft, casting a spell on him. Maybe she had collected his pubic hairs from the shower drain and toilet seat and she had constructed a voodoo doll that she was about to poke with a hairpin or lance with a knitting needle. He deserved it. Even after the beating he'd received from the pubescent hoodlums, he deserved it.

Or maybe Lena was painting her chewed fingernails in dazzling shades of pink and red, applying layers of makeup, trying on a big frilly dress and high heels, getting all tarted up for an imaginary date. She'd end up kissing a pillow, leaving bright smudges of makeup on the sheets. Simon stopped imagining when he remembered the dildo.

She'd hear him coming in, he thought, but he was hot and tired and didn't care. As he approached the door, her light flicked off, and he decided that he did care. He didn't want her to accost him again. Not tonight. He turned the key as quietly as he could and shook his flip-flop from his foot before he stepped onto the sticky linoleum.

The door to the basement was slightly ajar, allowing a hint of cool air to brush against

Simon's bare legs. It felt so good that he pulled the door all the way open and groped the painted cement wall for a light switch. The humidity of the night was gone, replaced with pleasant fresh air, like the woods on the first cold day in autumn.

Gardening implements—hedge clippers, hand shovels, an old black hose—hung from pegs screwed into the wall along the curving staircase. Simon softly closed the door behind him and walked down into the coolness. As he descended, the air seemed even cooler, fresher. He breathed it in, wanted to be cleaned from the inside out.

The cellar was immaculate, neat, despite its dirt floor. Shelves all along the walls held stacks and stacks of romance magazines. A hammock and its frame dominated the floor space. Simon imagined Lena luxuriating down there, the hammock swaying slightly as she read through her magazines. Maybe an open box of corn flakes on the floor within reach. While Aunt Lena seemed perfectly content in the scenario that Simon imagined, he couldn't help but feel sorry for her: a lonely woman in a basement, reading tales of other people's love, munching on bland corn flakes. Then, when he felt the dirt between his

raw toes, he remembered where he had been earlier: skulking around a deli worker's house like a
common criminal. He was more pathetic than
Lena. Way more.

He could no longer go to the municipal
swimming pool or the supermarket. He could
no longer walk down High Street. Maybe he
could grow a beard and start lifting weights.
Change his whole look by autumn.

Just as he flexed his meager biceps, he heard
Lena in the kitchen. Had he left the door to the
cellar stairs open? Was the light spilling out
into the kitchen?

Simon quickly hid under the stairs, squeezed
between some junk, and pulled a musty tarp
over his head. He heard the blood pumping
through his body, tried hard to slow his breathing, ignore the nervous bladder pressure that
ached through his gut.

Something was poking his kidney. His foot
hurt from walking home without a shoe. He felt
each of the blows he had received, especially the
ones to his face. One of those little wastoids
wore a ring. Probably Stevie.

Then he heard Aunt Lena on the basement
stairs, her heavy, labored steps thumping closer
and closer.

Simon clenched his eyes shut and listened as Lena shuffled around the dirt floor. She breathed heavily. It sounded as if something chunky was in her throat.

Finally he heard her ascending the stairs, but it was too late. The warm wetness had blossomed through his underpants and trickled down around his ankles. He hadn't wet his pants like that since he was a little kid, playing hide-and-seek with his cousins at their summer house in Cannon Beach. His weak bladder had earned him the nickname "Soakin' Simon" that summer. His cousin Bob, who was now a commodities broker in Maryland with two kids and a bitchy plastic-surgeried wife, still called him Soakin' Simon. Even addressed Christmas cards to Soakin' Simon.

Now he'd have to wait—at least an hour. She might go upstairs and check to see if he was in his bed asleep. She might just go upstairs and fall asleep herself. She might be sneaking back down to the basement, picking out the best knife, preparing to fillet Simon when he emerged from his hiding place.

• • •

The great-grandson of Urg Kis discovered the original designs in the family house in Medford.

Simon woke with a jolt, couldn't remember where he was. But his damp shorts reminded him of the whole disgusting night. He crawled out from under the tarp. Yellow morning sunshine pushed through the dusty windows and dimly lit the cellar like a hipster café. He felt hungover. His throat burned and scratched; he may have caught a summer cold. A buzzing head. A bruised body. One raw foot. And shorts full of piss.

Simon had been squatting between two stacks of thick books. When he opened the first of the dusty leather-bound tomes, he saw that it was his great-grandfather's work: type designs, on thick textured paper. As Simon flipped through the heavy pages, he wished he had learned more about type design and his great-grandfather's accomplishments. He did know a little about it: which typefaces his great-grandfather had designed, how he had been the talk of the typeface community in his day. It was money from his great-grandfather's trust that had paid for Simon's expensive undergraduate experience.

The same trust had put braces on Simon's teeth, allowed him to escape to camp for five summers, flown him to Europe, and bought him a Eurailpass after he graduated from college. Somehow, in the last six years, Simon had lost access to the money, actually had to borrow money to pay for grad school. His father had told him, "There are certain things that trust funds should be used for, and you've already done all of them."

The third book Simon picked up had the word *Surrendered* scrawled across the first page in faded red pen. The type was called Lena, which made Simon smile. The serifs were concave and splayed; the contrast between thick and thin strokes was marked. Dramatic. A beautiful type. A type that was actually familiar, probably used in many books Simon had read—but Simon had never known his grandfather was its designer. A weird familial pride welled up inside him. He wondered if his great-grandfather had named a type after anyone else in the family, and he began to flip through the remaining heavy books.

Simon didn't recognize the names of the other types in the stack—Burnham, Wellfort, Phoncolli, Octimingtone, Colonnaham, Dreit—but he recognized the actual types, knew he had them in his font bank on his computer. It made him think that there was a lot more money in that trust, money his father was greedily hoarding or giving to Brian.

The typeface's original name was "Lena," named for Kis's granddaughter.

The second stack of books was different. The type designs were replaced with proof pages of magazines and booklets. Yellowed black-and-whites. Pornography. A series of photographs depicting young Lena and a blond boy pleasuring each other with the wooden dildo.

When Simon reached the end of the first book, his fingertips numb, he had seen things he had only heard or read about—all the *philias* he had once memorized for a quiz in an abnormal psychology class he took as an undergraduate.

He paused every so often, when he saw something confusing or amazing—sexual contortions, gynecological close-ups, degrading ejaculations—and he held the book up to the light, but never for more than a few seconds. He kept going. Driven. Searching, tossing the books to the side, sweat coursing down his back, his heart racing, his mouth dry and foul-tasting. He felt guilty, especially after last night's antics, but the guilt was exciting and he kept going, acquiescing to the eager fluttering in his gut and his tingling half-erection.

More books. More photographs. More depraved. Costumes: Indians, Sailors, Kitty Cats, Babies. Clamps, butt-plugs, straps, metal stirrups, speculums, multi-headed dildonic devices, scat play.

Just as Simon closed the last book in the stack, he looked up to see Lena standing on the stairs in her robe and fuzzy slippers. His stomach suddenly felt empty.

"I knew the minute you first walked into my house," Lena said, stepping down into the dirt.

"Oh," Simon said. He could smell his own piss, and he wondered if Lena could. "I was just looking at the old type designs." His voice quivered. He felt as if he might wet his shorts again, like all the muscles in his abdomen had instantly atrophied and collapsed.

"I knew," she said. "I saw it in your eyes, in the way you stand, the way you move."

Simon's eyes burned. His mouth tasted metallic.

"And I knew I'd find you down here one of these days." Her squinted left eye opened completely, matched her right eye. "I knew you'd eventually be drawn down here." She sat on the stairs. Breathed heavily for a few moments, then she said, "A lock wouldn't have done any good."

"I'm not a pervert," Simon said. "If that's what you think."

"It'll eventually get you into trouble," Lena said. "Like it did your great-grandfather."

"Stop it!" Simon said, his eyes glazing over with wetness.

"Once Jessup's father found out about the tableaux, it was all over." Aunt Lena sat on the stairs, arranged her fatness like she was preparing to tell Simon a long story.

He didn't want to hear it. "Please stop," he said.

"I'm not judging you," Lena said. "I loved grandpa. I loved everything about him, even his prurience."

Simon wanted to run away, but Lena, sitting on the stairs, was blocking his egress.

"The blond boy in the photos you looked at,"

Lena said. "That was Jessup. He was my boy-friend outside the pictures, too, you know."

Simon needed a shower. He needed to sleep. He was hungry, too, and his bruises hurt. That didn't concern him, though. "It's a perfectly normal response for someone to open books they find," Simon choked out. Then he began to babble: "Not that I own any, but most men my age own some pornography, whether it's a few videotapes, some magazines, or a folder of downloads on their computer. It's normal."

"Jessup's last name was Wayland," Lena said. "You can probably figure out why your great-grandfather had to sign away his last type designs."

"Especially men. Men are more turned on visually than women. So when it comes down to it, I wasn't really doing anything out of the ordinary down here."

"He cried, you know," Lena said. "He cried when he told me."

"I was merely being a normal man my age. Doing what a normal man my age would do if he discovered several books of pornography. I just looked at them. Is that a crime? Does that make me some sort of sexual deviant?"

• • •

The legal documents showing the Wayland foundry as the sole owner of the typeface proved to be in order and were upheld in the Massachusetts courts when challenged by members of the Kis family.

Now Simon is home, in Portland, Oregon, driving his mother's station wagon to the Safeway supermarket on Halsey. Going to see Sheila, who works the deli, who slices turkey fresh for Simon, who still smells of lunch meats when she goes to church across town after her early shift on Sunday morning. Sheila is like a big baby, Simon thinks. She is pudgy. Her knuckles are dimpled, and her skin is pink and fresh. Her red hair is cut short. She smiles a lot.

Sheila's boyfriend lives only two blocks from Simon's parents. His name, Simon thinks, is Donald. He works at an Irish pub on Hawthorne, closer to where Sheila lives with her sister, Mary, on the second floor of a brown duplex with well-groomed shrubs.

• • •

While the Wayland family still owns the typeface, it was proven irrefutably in court by the
great-grandson of Urg Kis that it is indeed a Kis
type.

Today is the day Simon will introduce himself to
Sheila. They chat briefly every Monday and
Thursday anyway, and as far as Simon can see,
Donald doesn't treat Sheila right, doesn't open
the car door for her, doesn't give her free
Guinness pints at the pub where he works, didn't
buy her anything nice for Saint Valentine's
Day—just a cheap bouquet of spring flowers, not
roses, and Portland is the City of Roses.

But as Simon looks up the street toward Safeway, he notices something that sickens him,
something that causes him to swerve the station
wagon to the side of the road and wipe the sweat
that has just beaded on his brow. A new bright
billboard: News Center 12. His brother, Brian,
smiling in his perfect suit, gigantic, looking at
Simon. I'm the young handsome weatherman
whom Portland loves, Brian says, and you're a
pervert.

MARK JUDE POIRIER is a graduate of Georgetown, Stanford, the Writing Seminars at John Hopkins, and the Iowa Writers' Workshop. The author of *Naked Pueblo* and *Goats*, he recently was awarded a Chesterfield screenwriting fellowship with Paramount Pictures. He lives in Los Angeles, California and Archer City, Texas.